At Issue

Genetically Modified Food

Other Books in the At Issue Series:

At Issue

I Genetically Modified Food

Diane Andrews Henningfield, Book Editor

GREENHAVEN PRESS
A part of Gale, Cengage Learning

GALE
CENGAGE Learning

Detroit • New York • San Francisco • New Haven, Conn • Waterville, Maine • London

Christine Nasso, *Publisher*
Elizabeth Des Chenes, *Managing Editor*

© 2009 Greenhaven Press, a part of Gale, Cengage Learning.

Gale and Greenhaven Press are registered trademarks used herein under license.

For more information, contact:
Greenhaven Press
27500 Drake Rd.
Farmington Hills, MI 48331-3535
Or you can visit our Internet site at gale.cengage.com

For product information and technology assistance, contact us at

Gale Customer Support, 1-800-877-4253
For permission to use material from this text or product, submit all requests online at www.cengage.com/permissions

Further permissions questions can be emailed to permissionrequest@cengage.com

Articles in Greenhaven Press anthologies are often edited for length to meet page requirements. In addition, original titles of these works are changed to clearly present the main thesis and to explicitly indicate the author's opinion. Every effort is made to ensure that Greenhaven Press accurately reflects the original intent of the authors. Every effort has been made to trace the owners of copyrighted material.

Cover image copyright Debra Hughes 2007. Used under license from Shutterstock.com.

LIBRARY OF CONGRESS CATALOGING-IN-PUBLICATION DATA

Genetically modified food / Diane Andrews Henningfield, book editor.
    p. cm. -- (At issue)
  Includes bibliographical references and index.
  ISBN 978-0-7377-4098-1 (hardcover)
  ISBN 978-0-7377-4099-8 (pbk.)
  1. Genetically modified foods. I. Henningfield, Diane Andrews. II. Series: At issue (San Diego, Calif.)
  TP248.65.F66G4574 2009
  363.19'29--dc22

                                                    2008029477

Printed in the United States of America
1 2 3 4 5 6 7 12 11 10 09 08

Contents

Introduction

In the last decades of the twentieth century, scientists learned to manipulate the genetic code, or DNA, of various plants and animals. By splicing the DNA from one organism into the DNA of a second organism, scientists were able to pass a trait from the first organism to the second. For example, a researcher might isolate a gene that prevents mildew and rot in beans and splice it into tomatoes, producing a tomato that looks and tastes just like a traditionally grown tomato, but which is resistant to mildew and rot. Such a tomato would be tastier for consumers and more profitable for the business that grows it.

On one hand, such gene-splicing opens a whole world of possibilities for the improvement of food. Food that is resistant to disease and drought could one day feed the hungry of the world, supporters of genetically modified food argue. Opponents, however, fear that genetically modified food might not be safe and could also destroy traditional agriculture and biodiversity. Advocates of genetic engineering of food argue that large corporations and philanthropic organizations are freely giving away much-needed food. Critics protest that these multinational agribusinesses are trying to monopolize the market through genetic engineering in order to make even more money.

The story of Golden Rice encapsulates many of the controversies and issues surrounding the production of genetically modified food. Many people around the world depend on rice as the primary staple of their diets. Historically, rice was consumed with its outer layer intact. Today, this kind of rice is called "brown rice." However, brown rice quickly becomes rancid during storage. Polishing the rice, a technology developed in modern times, produces a rice that remains tasty even after long storage. However, most of the nutrients found in rice are located in the outer covering, or bran, which is lost through polishing. Consequently, throughout the world, people who depend largely on white rice for food often develop serious health problems due to the lack of proper nutrition. According to C.S. Prakash and Gregory Conko, writing for the March 1, 2004 issue of *AgBio World*, "The diet of more than 3 billion people worldwide includes inadequate levels of essential vitamins and minerals such as Vitamin A and iron. Deficiency in just these two micronutrients can result in severe anemia, impaired intellectual development, blindness and even death."

Recognizing this, scientists—supported by the Rockefeller Foundation and the multinational agribusiness Syngenta, along with the Philippine Rice Institute—decided to work on increasing the available Vitamin A in rice. In 1999, professors Peter Beyer and Ingo Portrykus were successful in producing a prototype of a rice that had a much higher beta carotene content, providing increased levels of Vitamin A. They called their creation "Golden Rice." The scientists knew that in order for the rice to have any effect on world health, however, it would have to be inexpensive and available to farmers. Therefore, according to Erin Baggott in the Fall 2006 *Harvard International Review*, "The Golden Rice Humanitarian Board and Syngenta . . . proposed to donate Golden Rice seeds to subsistence farmers earning less than US$10,000 a year."

Here the group encountered the first of many controversies surrounding Golden Rice: They needed to obtain permission from the many people who owned patents and intellectual property rights on the technology that made Golden Rice possible. The issue of patents and ownership of genetically modified organisms has since become a contentious issue for all developers of genetically modified food. As Jerry Cayford writes in the Winter 2004 *Issues in Science and Technology*, many critics of biotechnology are not opposed to genetically modified food; rather, "they are opposed to the patenting of plants, which biotechnology makes possible. They consider this new expansion of the patent system to be an ill-conceived transfer of the raw materials of all food production from the public domain to private control."

The question of ownership was not the only problem for the distribution of Golden Rice. As Elena Conis writes in the October 22, 2007, *Los Angeles Times*, "Opponents call [genetically modified foods] Frankenfoods, man-made aberrations that should be banished from our grocery stores or at least clearly labeled so consumers know what they're eating." Organizations such as Greenpeace worked actively against the development of genetically modified food such as Golden Rice. According to Baggott, "[Non-governmental organizations] like Greenpeace and Friends of the Earth have crystallized Europe's general anti-GM sentiment into a direct criticism of Golden Rice." These groups charge that the rice, like all genetically modified foods, might not be safe for human consumption. In addition, they believe that it will damage biodiversity. Finally, they assert that it might make malnutrition worse rather than better, since people might stop eating vegetables once they have Golden Rice.

Scientists in 2004 conducted a successful field trial of Golden Rice in Louisiana. However, the issues surrounding genetically modified food have hindered the intended distribution of the rice. For those who believe Golden Rice can save eyesight and lives, it is a tragedy. As Derek Hanekom writes in the South African edition of *Business Day*, August 2, 2006, "Africa's food insecurity means developing agriculture is an important objective. Genetic modfication technologies—with a potential for pest resistance, drought and herbicide tolerance, as well as improved nutritional characteristics—must surely be part of the solution." On the other hand, opponents want to delay or prevent the distribution of Golden Rice and other genetically modified foods. As a July 10, 2007 article in the *East African* reports, "small-scale Kenyan farmers have expressed suspicions that the ongoing campaign to have the country adopt GMOs is a subtle scheme by giant multinationals to get them 'hooked' to the latter's seeds and anti-pest chemicals, thus creating a huge market for them." Because there are compelling arguments on both sides of the issue, it is important to read widely and deeply before forming an opinion.

The viewpoints that follow examine closely the many controversial issues surrounding the genetic engineering of food. From health concerns to environmental claims, genetically modified food promises to be a hotly contested topic for years to come.

1

An Overview of the Genetically Modified Food Debate

Valeria Jefferson

Valeria Jefferson is a corresponding author for the Journal of Environmental Health *and is the president of the National Capital Area Environmental Health Association located in Clinton, Maryland.*

When scientists change the genetic makeup of a plant or animal in order to produce desirable traits in the organism, they are engaging in what is called genetic modification. The resulting plants, animals, or microorganisms are called genetically modified organisms (GMOs); when GMOs are used for food, they're known as genetically modified foods (GMFs). Scientists, environmentalists, political analysts, and consumers debate whether genetic modification ought to be allowed. Proponents argue that GMFs can help solve the problems of hunger and environmental pollution. Opponents counter that GMOs pose a serious health risk to humans and cause irreversible genetic pollution. Both sides are trying to answer whether the benefits of GMFs outweigh the possible negative consequences.

With an ever-increasing global population, hunger in the developing world, and the health risks of pesticides, some experts view genetically modified food as a panacea. Others view it as one of the most serious threats to human

Valeria Jefferson, "The Ethical Dilemma of Genetically Modified Food," *Journal of Environmental Health*, vol. 69, no. 1, July–August 2006, pp. 33–34. Copyright © National Environmental Health Association. Reproduced by permission.

civilization. The These diametrically opposing views point to an ethical dilemma, that will certainly be difficult to resolve: whether the benefits of developing and supplying the world with genetically modified foods outweigh future consequences that these products may have for the human species, animal life, and the ecosystem.

Plant and animal modification is not a new concept. Before genetic engineering, gene modification was accomplished through breeding. The traditional breeding method ultimately produces the same desired effect as genetic engineering, but it occurs over a much longer time span and is self-limiting. Selected individual genes are transferred from one organism to another between plants and between animals, but not between plants and animals. Through genetic engineering, genes can be transferred between any organisms: A hypothetical example might be a gene from a fish that lives in cold seas being inserted into a strawberry so that the strawberry could survive frost.

Genetic engineering (GE) belongs to the field of biotechnology, which is the science governing genetic modification, genetic engineering, genetic manipulation, other gene technologies, and recombinant-DNA technology. Recently, use of biotechnology has expanded from the pharmaceutical and medical industries into the agricultural industry.

Genetically Modified Organisms (GMOs) Explained

The collective term "genetically modified organisms," or GMOs, is used frequently in regulatory documents and in the scientific literature to describe "plants, animals and microorganisms which have had DNA introduced into them by means other than by combination of an egg and a sperm or by natural bacterial conjugation" [according to the Institute of Food Science and Technology]. For instance, the genetic makeup of plants can be altered to produce insect-resistant plants. Genetic engineering may also produce animals, plants, or bacteria that contain desired nutrients.

In spite of the common good offered by GMF, opponents argue that gene manipulation is unsafe.

Despite government approval of genetically modified foods in the nation's foods supply, genetically modified food (GMF) does pose philosophical problems. Opponents argue that government agencies are violating their religious and consumer rights, while proponents have taken a utilitarian approach, arguing that the economic and social benefits of GMF far outweigh any possible negative consequences. Utilitarian ethics hold that the rightness of an action entirely depends on the value of its consequences, and that the usefulness can be rationally estimated. Increased productivity and the usefulness of GMF appear to be the driving force rationalizing this new technology.

GMFs May Solve World Hunger

Genetically modified foods grow faster and larger than non-GMFs and may be more resistant to pests, heat, cold, and drought. They also help the environment by reducing pesticide and herbicide use. Other far-reaching goals are envisioned for GMF, such as stopping the hunger problem in developing countries. Over 800 million people in the world are chronically or severely malnourished. Many eat less than the minimum quantity necessary for survival, resulting in a mortality rate of 36 million deaths per year. Somewhere in the world, a child dies every seven seconds, and the cause of death is directly or indirectly attributable to hunger. In hunger-stricken areas, malnourished women are iron deficient; in poorer countries, 50 percent of pregnant women suffer from iron deficiency, a condition responsible for nearly 20 percent of maternal deaths. In addition to alleviating world hunger, the production of GMF can easily meet agricultural demands associated with population increase. There will be approximately 1.5 billion more people in the world in the next 20 years, and what better way to keep up with agricultural demand than with GMF? In spite of the common good offered by GMF, opponents argue that gene manipulation is unsafe. Genetically modified food may have harmful effects on animals, ecosystems, and humans, and these effects may be irreversible.

The Debate Over Genetically Modified Food

The debate over genetically modified food originated in the early 1980s. Concerns range from ethical issues related to the long-term health effects of eating GMF to the detrimental effects gene manipulation may have on animals and the ecosystem. In the book *Vexing Nature*, Gary Comstock (2000) describes two ethically derived objections to genetic engineering: intrinsic and extrinsic.

Those who intrinsically object to GMF believe [according to Gary Comstock] that "it is unnatural to genetically engineer plants, animals and foods." Extrinsic objections focus on the potential to cause harm. These effects may be irreversible. Animals may suffer as a result of genetic modifications or modifications to their genetic material. The component of hereditary material, or germ plasm, that specifies characteristics of different cells may be lost through bioengineering. Comstock justifies the suffering and death of research animals using the "Miniride Principle (MP)." The MP holds that "where comparable harms are involved, override the fewest individuals' rights." The MP justifies production and killing of genetically modified animals provided that the research addresses comparable harms for the research subjects and human life. For instance, MP would not justify the production and killing of genetically modified mice to study human hair loss. The loss of human hair is not considered to be life threatening.

Do Chemicals of GMFs Cause More Environmental Harm?

The question becomes whether the damage that has been perpetuated upon the environment through the use of pesticides and harmful chemicals causes more damage to the environment than the narrowing of the germ plasm through the development of GMFs. [According to the U.S. Department of Agriculture]:

> The high societal costs associated with rapid destruction of natural habitats and agricultural productive capacity may be most extreme in the developing countries of the tropics, where a wealth of genetic resources vital to U.S. agriculture is endangered. Greater emphasis should be placed on conservation of germplasm through international cooperation. Development and maintenance of stable biological communities in the natural environment should be a high priority goal worldwide.

Should we be ending hunger by causing genetic mutations we have not anticipated, or moving toward the goal of ending world hunger safely through application of sound scientific principles?

The proliferation of biogenetic plants also poses a concern. The pollen produced by these plants, carrying new genes, cannot be contained. As a result, genetic pollution of natural crop varieties and of wild plant relatives may occur. Genetic pollution may result from accidental or deliberate release of genetically engineered bacteria, insects, fish, and other life forms into the environment. Unlike other forms of pollution, as Michael Fox points out in his book *Beyond Evolution*, genetic pollution is uncontrollable, irreversible, and permanent, posing a major threat to biodiversity and to the bio-integrity of the entire life community.

Benefits and Dangers

Food bio-engineering is a powerful and promising technology that offers both benefits and dangers to modern society. An enormous number of changes can be made through molecular manipulation. Biotechnology research should proceed with precautionary principles in mind. Biotech engineers should ask themselves the following questions: Is this new technology necessary, safe, and effective? Is it traceable—can the product be recalled if necessary? Can it be regulated and, if so, at what cost to society? What are the long- and short-term effects on the ecosystem, on the structure of agriculture here and abroad, and on animal welfare? These are just some of the questions Fox outlines in his bioethical criteria for acceptability. The ethics of preserving the earth's bio-integrity must direct and constrain genetic engineering.

The consequences of moving forward too rapidly without a full accounting of the possible adverse impacts are staggering. At the same time, I recognize that there is a need to advance technologically and that those advances could result in an end to world hunger. But what is the most important consideration? Should we be ending hunger by causing genetic mutations we have not anticipated, or moving toward the goal of ending world hunger safely through application of sound scientific principles?

2

Genetically Modified Foods Are Safe

Jon Entine

Jon Entine is a documentary producer and writer on public policy issues. He is an adjunct fellow at the American Enterprise Institute for Public Policy Research and writes on sustainability and corporate ethics.

The European Union (EU) has restricted genetically modified (GM) crops purportedly because of safety and environmental concerns. The World Trade Organization, however, states that the ban is not based on scientific research, but on an attempt by the ᴇU to protect its farmers from American imports. Scientific research shows that GM foods can provide needed nourishment to developing countries, and that there are no documented health risks. Science has also demonstrated that GM crops can be raised safely with less impact on the environment than traditionally raised crops. In spite of documented GM food safety, the work of anti-GM food activists threatens to deny the children of the world the benefit of biotechnology.

Call it "the spin wars". In a leaked interim report in February [2006] the World Trade Organisation [WTO] sided with Canada, Argentina, and the US, ruling that the European-wide ban on bio-engineered crops has more to do with protectionism than precaution. But that's not what you'd believe if you relied on the hysteria-grams flooding the internet.

Jon Entine, "Debate: Genetically Modified Food and the WTO Ruling—Let Them Eat Precaution: What the WTO Decision on GMOs Really Means," *Ethical Corporation*, April 2006. www.ethicalcorp.com. Reproduced by permission.

Greenpeace blasted the WTO as "unqualified to deal with complex scientific and environmental issues". Friends of the Earth scowled "European safeguards" were being "sacrificed to benefit biotech corporations". The Consumers Union lambasted the "pre-emptive effort to chill the development of new policies for regulating GM [genetically modified] crops". The WTO, they chorused, is a puppet of nefarious biotechnology corporations aligned with bully nations force-feeding Europe with "Frankenfoods".

Let's separate the chaff from the wheat. If this 1,045-page report is upheld, Europe will not have to alter a single regulation or label. Consumers will not be forced to buy and eat food that they do not want. The WTO will demand the EU [European Union] observe its own regulations—using sound science to evaluate new products. That has not been happening. European countries have been exploiting the controversy to protect their farmers and keep prices high.

Anti-GMO campaigners have been on the attack since the first generation of biotech crops—soybeans, wheat, cotton, and canola that generate natural insecticides, making them more resistant to pests and drought and reducing reliance on environmentally harmful chemicals—were introduced more than a decade ago. Why? Primarily because corporations brought them to market.

GMOs Are a Solution to Malnutrition

We are now entering the second phase of the revolution— addressing malnutrition and aiding smaller farmers. Nutrition-enhanced foods such as "Golden Rice" could help millions of malnourished children suffering from vitamin A deficiency. On the horizon are futuristic "farmaceuticals"—medicines made by melding basic agriculture with advanced biotechnology, creating new foods, such as potatoes transformed into edible vaccines against diarrhoea, a leading cause of death in the developing world.

Yet, in a dark, parallel universe of the privileged, egged on by "ethical investors" and funded by the organic and natural product industries, which thrive on food scares, protestors cite the lowest common denominator in fabricated scientific disputes: the "precautionary principle"—the controversial notion that innovations should be shelved unless all risks can be avoided.

They assert "Trojan Horse" genes could unleash a "genetic Godzilla", causing environmental havoc.

Slogans like "better safe than sorry" may ring of moderation, but they are simplistic. The WTO acknowledged as much, ruling there is no mainstream scientific support for the precautionary principle, but leaving the door open to handling the GMO issue differently "if new scientific evidence comes to light which conflicts with available scientific evidence".

Noting that biotech crops are just as safe and healthy as conventional crops . . . the United Nations has urged their extension to the developing world.

Every activity involves risk. Conventional farmers use chemicals that have unknown long-term consequences. Should we ban conventionally grown foods? People die and fall ill eating organic foods caused by fecal contamination from dung—a "natural" fertilizer. Should we remove these products from the shelves? We are not about to stop vaccinating infants because of the unfounded fear that inoculations cause harm. Do we really want to make profound decisions not on the basis of what we know but on the basis of what we do not know?

There have been no documented health problems linked to GM crops and no evidence that genetic modification poses greater risks than crossbreeding and gene-splicing, which have given us such products as the tangelo and seedless grape. Noting that biotech crops are just as safe and healthy as conventional crops, and can be grown with less environmental hazard, the United Nations has urged their extension to the developing world.

Back on their heels, anti-GMO groups have attempted to reframe the debate in starkly political terms, citing the Biosafety Protocol, which Greenpeace claims should allow countries "to ban or restrict the import and use of GE [genetically engineered] organisms when there is a lack of scientific knowledge or consensus regarding their safety". But this "international law" is actually only an extra-legal declaration.

The hypothetical risk of biotechnology has to be balanced against the lives lost because new [genetically modified] products remain trapped in a regulatory maze.

The WTO saw through this hyperbole, pointedly writing: "There has been to date no authoritative decision by an international court or tribunal which recognises the precautionary principle as a principle of general or customary international law". Should the Biosafety Protocol become law, studies have shown it would be a disaster for developing countries (and a boon for protectionist-minded Europe).

The hypothetical risk of biotechnology has to be balanced against the lives lost because new products remain trapped in a regulatory maze. In 2002, Zambia and Zimbabwe, wary of offending their major trading partners in the EU, cited the "precautionary principle" in rejecting donations of bioengineered grain that could have helped feed ten million undernourished people, thousands of whom ultimately died.

Today in the Philippines, where 42% of the diet comes from white rice, a study by UN food experts estimates that "Golden Rice" could avert 879 deaths, 1,925 corneal ulcers, and 15,398 cases of night blindness each year. A Philippine-based anti-biotechnology group with ties to Greenpeace has aggressively lobbied against "Golden Rice" on the grounds that the benefits from beta-carotene are minimal—claims rejected by scientists.

GM Food Is Popular with the People

We should also be sceptical of polls suggesting consumers, particularly in Europe, are dead set against these innovations. "If you really want to understand whether European shoppers will buy genetically modified foods given the opportunity, ignore the agents provocateurs, the media, and the panicked reactions of the big supermarket chains, and look instead at the behaviour of [the] ordinary consumer," says David Bowe of the European Parliament's committee on environment, public health and consumer policy. "When Safeway and Sainsbury's put GM tomato purée side by side with their non-GM counterparts in 1999 the proof was definitely in the purée. The GM product was seen to offer real added value. It was less expensive and in numerous blind tastings consumers seemed to prefer the flavour. It sold as well as the non-GM product".

The biggest losers are the children, frozen out of the benefits of the green revolution that many of us take for granted.

Even with this WTO ruling, political realities suggest this subterfuge may not end soon. Greece and Hungary recently announced they would defy EU regulations and broaden their bans on GM maize seeds, citing "toxicity". No scientific research was presented to back up this allegation.

While not a silver bullet, GM technology offers unique tools to address international food needs. Biotech crops are grown mostly in major farming nations but farmers in developing countries such as Brazil, China, India, and in Eastern Europe, with hungry stomachs to feed, are vigorously embracing the technology. Last year, 8.5 million farmers in 21 countries grew biotech crops on 222 million acres, an 11% year-on-year increase.

There are valid concerns, including the degree to which corporations should be allowed to patent beneficial seeds, keeping in mind that Monsanto, Bayer, Novartis and other firms need to recoup their development costs, which have multiplied exponentially because of the country-by-country, complex and repetitive approval process.

But years of demagoguery have taken an enormous toll—polluting public opinion, profoundly altering the trajectory of biotechnology applications and damaging the financial wherewithal of corporations and university research projects. The biggest losers are the children, frozen out of the benefits of the green revolution that many of us take for granted.

3

The Health Risks of Genetically Modified Foods Are Being Ignored

Jeffrey M. Smith

Jeffrey M. Smith is the director of the Institute for Responsible Technology. He is the author of Seeds of Deception *(2003) and* Genetic Roulette *(2007).*

The United States Food and Drug Administration (FDA) does not require safety tests on genetically modified (GM) food in spite of warnings from scientists of potential health risks. Despite claims that GM food is safe, very few animal feeding studies, and only one study on the effects of GM food on humans, have been conducted. In addition, while it is possible that GM food is already causing serious health problems, it may take decades for the link between health problems and GM food to be made. By the time a link is established, it will be too late to prevent serious consequences.

When Kirk Azevedo accepted a Monsanto Company recruiter's offer in 1996 to sell genetically modified (GM) crops, it wasn't the pay increase that inspired him. It was the writings of Monsanto CEO Robert Shapiro that were his motivation. Shapiro had painted a picture of feeding the world and cleaning up the environment with his company's new technology. Kirk was fascinated by the idea of swapping

Jeffrey M. Smith, "Introduction: Deceptions, Assumptions, and Denial—Exposing the Roots of Genetically Modified Crops," *Genetic Roulette: The Documented Health Risks of Genetically Engineered Foods*, Fairfield, IA: Yes! Books, 2007, pp. 1–3, 10–11.

genes between species, creating designer organisms that could reduce manufacturing waste, turning "fields into factories and producing anything from lifesaving drugs to insect-resistant plants" [as he wrote in 2006]. When he visited Monsanto's St. Louis headquarters for new employee training, Azevedo shared his enthusiasm for Shapiro's vision during a meeting. When the session ended, a company vice president pulled him aside and set him straight.

"Wait a second," he told Azevedo. "What Robert Shapiro says is one thing. But what we do is something else. We are here to make money. He is the front man who tells a story. We don't even understand what he is saying."

Scientists agreed that genetic engineering leads to "different risks" than traditional breeding and . . . repeatedly warned their superiors that [genetically modified] foods might create unpredictable, hard-to-detect side effects.

Azevedo was jolted. His image "of helping and healing" the world through GM crops turned out to be a manufactured reality—a lie—crafted to gain public acceptance and to push products. Azevedo realized he was working for "just another profit-oriented company."

The Food and Drug Administration Hides the Truth

Helping the world is only one of several manufactured realities about GM crops, the most fundamental of which is that the foods are safe. The key source for this claim is the United States Food and Drug Administration (FDA). According to their 1992 policy on GM foods, "The agency is not aware of any information showing that foods derived by these new methods differ from other foods in any meaningful or uniform way." On the basis of that sentence, the FDA claimed that no safety studies are necessary and that "Ultimately, it is the food producer who is responsible for assuring safety." Biotech companies thus determine on their own if their products are harmless. This policy set the stage for the rapid deployment of the new technology. The seed industry was consolidated, millions of acres were planted, hundreds of millions were fed, consumers and nations objected, laws were passed, crops were contaminated, billions of dollars were lost—and it turns out that sentence was a lie.

The FDA was *fully* aware that GM crops were meaningfully different. That, in fact, was the overwhelming consensus among "the technical experts in the agency" [as stated by Linda Kahl of the Alliance for Bio-Integrity]. The scientists agreed that genetic engineering leads to "different risks" than traditional breeding and had repeatedly warned their superiors that GM foods might create unpredictable, hard-to-detect side effects. They urged the political appointees who were in charge at the FDA to require long-term safety studies, including human studies, to guard against possible allergies, toxins, new diseases, and nutritional problems.

GM varieties that have never been fed to animals in rigorous safety studies and probably never fed to humans at all are approved for sale in grocery stores.

The scientists' concerns were kept secret in 1992, when FDA policy was put into place. But seven years later, internal records were made public due to a lawsuit and the deception came to light. The agency's newly released 44,000 pages revealed that government scientists' "references to the unintended negative effects . . . were progressively deleted from drafts of the policy statement (over the protests of agency scientists)" [according to Steven M. Druker of the Alliance for Bio-Integrity]. They further revealed that the FDA was under orders from the White House to promote GM crops and that Michael Taylor, Monsanto's former attorney and later its vice president, was brought into the FDA to oversee policy development. With Taylor in charge, the scientists' warnings were ignored and denied.

Untested GM Food for Sale

As a result, consultation with the FDA on GM food safety is a voluntary exercise, in which the agency receives summaries without data and conclusions without foundation. If the company claims that its foods are safe, the FDA has no further questions. Thus, GM varieties that have never been fed to animals in rigorous safety studies and probably *never* fed to humans at all are approved for sale in grocery stores.

In the mid-1990s, the UK [United Kingdom] government decided to institute what US leaders refused to—rigorous, long-term safety testing. They commissioned scientists to develop an assessment protocol for GM crop approvals that would be used in the UK and eventually by the EU. In 1998, three years into the project, the scientists discovered that potatoes engineered to produce a harmless insecticide caused extensive health damage to rats. The pro-GM government immediately canceled the project, the lead scientist was fired and the research team dismantled. The assessment requirements that were eventually adopted by the EU were a far cry from those that were being developed in the UK. The superficial testing schemes still have yet to meet the demands of the FDA's stifled scientists.

Few GM Safety Studies Have Been Conducted

Ironically, policy makers around the world gain confidence in the safety of GM crops because they wrongly assume that the US FDA has approved them based on extensive tests, and approvals everywhere rely on the developers to do safety studies on their own crops. Research does not need to be published and most is kept secret under the guise of "confidential business information." Very little data is available for public scrutiny. In 2003, for example, researchers [Ian F. Pryme and Rolf Lembcke in *Nutrition and Health*] reviewed published, peer-reviewed animal feeding studies that qualified as safety assessments. There were ten. The correlation between the findings and the funding was telling. Five studies "performed more or less in collaboration with private companies" reported no adverse effects. In the three independent studies, "adverse effects were reported." The authors said, "It is remarkable that these effects have all been observed after feeding for only 10–14 days."

Biotech advocates claim that there is plenty of evidence for safety. In December 2004, for example, Christopher Preston did a database search of peer-reviewed animal feeding studies worldwide and came up with 41. Although this is still an incredibly low number of papers by which to judge safety, according to Arpad Pusztai, an expert in feeding studies, Preston's list failed "to distinguish between a scientific study and an animal production exercise." The latter "may be of some value to commercial animal production but have limited scientific value." When the commercial studies were removed from the list, it left only 18 (4 of which are in Russian or Chinese).

GM foods might already be contributing to serious, widespread health problems, but since no one is monitoring for this, it could take decades to identify.

In October 2005, Wayne Parrot compiled 60 abstracts entitled "General Safety and Safety Assessment of Specific Genetically Modified Crops from Scientific Journal Articles." The list was presented to the minister for agriculture and food in the government of western Australia as evidence that sufficient research had been conducted to conclude that GM food was safe. According to an analysis by epidemiologist Judy Carman, "A review of these abstracts found that most were animal production studies. . . . In fact, only nine abstracts could be considered to contain measures applicable to human health. The majority of these (six abstracts; 67%) found adverse effects from eating GM crops." Carman pointed out that several other studies with adverse findings had been omitted from the compilation. She concluded, "The list of abstracts therefore does not support claims that GM crops are safe to eat. On the contrary, it provides evidence that GM crops may be harmful to health."

Bad Science

By the beginning of 2007, there were just over 20 peer-reviewed animal feeding safety studies on GM crops. Only a single human feeding trial has been published and there is no post-marketing surveillance on those eating GM foods. Trials funded or conducted by the GM crop producers, however, are consistently substandard. They typically fail to investigate the impacts of GM food on gut function, liver function, kidney function, the immune system, the endocrine system, blood composition, allergic response, effects on the unborn, the potential to cause cancer, or impacts on gut bacteria. In addition, the industry-funded studies have become notorious for using creative ways to avoid finding problems. They feed older animals instead of more sensitive young ones, keep sample sizes too low to achieve the statistical significance needed for proof in scientific studies, dilute the GM component of the feed, overcook samples, compare results with irrelevant controls, choose obsolete insensitive detection methods, limit the duration of feeding trials, and even ignore animal deaths and sickness. They've got "bad science" down to a science. . . .

One of the most unscientific and dangerous statements made by biotech proponents is that millions of people in the US have been eating GM food for a decade and no one has gotten sick. On the contrary, GM foods might already be contributing to serious, widespread health problems, but since no one is monitoring for this, it could take decades to identify.

GM Food Health Problems Could Take Decades to Surface

Judy Carman, a former senior epidemiologist for the government of South Australia, describes the difficulties from a public health perspective. "The first problem is to recognize that there is a new health problem in the community. Without full animal testing, we don't even know which diseases to look for in people." If GM crops created a *new* disease, it would not have an established surveillance system. In fact, most *existing* diseases do not have any effective surveillance systems in place, making it hard to identify a change.

Carman points out that, "The HIV/AIDS epidemic went unnoticed for decades, even though it created memorable secondary infections . . . and had a focus in young gay men who tended to cluster geographically and see the same doctors. It was largely picked-up by chance . . . even though there were by then thousands of HIV/AIDS cases worldwide."

Once a new disease (or increased incidence of an existing disease) is identified, it must be tracked to its cause. Carman says, "Anything that looks like an infectious disease usually results in an investigation by a state or local health authority. Anything else, for example, an increase in cancer, relies on someone, usually an academic, having an interest in the disease and applying in a competitive medical research grant system, for funding to do the investigation." That could take years. If a research effort is funded, "For an existing disease, existing hypotheses would be considered and tested before GM foods, creating a delay in finding the cause," says Carman.

"Then people would need to accurately remember what they had been eating. Most people cannot even remember everything they ate the day before." Moreover, GM foods in many countries, including the United States, are not labeled.

Neither consumers nor manufacturers know how much GM content is in the food. "So how can an investigator properly investigate and hence expose the link between the GM food and the illness?" Carman concludes that it "may be almost impossible to prove that a GM food has caused a disease, even if there are thousands of cases."

Tracking GM Food's Effects Is Difficult

Some of the difficulties of tracking a GM food's effects were witnessed when StarLink, a GM corn variety unapproved for human consumption, contaminated the US food supply. The concern was that the properties of StarLink's GM protein may trigger allergic reactions. But even with a recall affecting more than three hundred brands and a major disruption of US corn exports, the investigation mounted by the FDA to determine whether the food was allergenic was miserable.

[Epidemiologist Judy Carman] points out. . . . "Even if a GM food is found to cause harm, it may take many years of effort to remove it from the food supply."

The agency established only a passive monitoring system, contacting and testing only the tiny percentage of affected people who filed formal complaints with them. They never investigated the thousands of health-related consumer calls made to food companies, including those who were rushed to the hospital. The FDA also failed to contact health professionals or allergy groups around the country. It took them nine months to prepare an allergenicity test, but it was so poorly designed, the EPA's expert panel on allergies rejected its conclusions.

A Deadly Epidemic

The deadly epidemic caused by the GM food supplement L-Tryptophan [in the 1980s] is another demonstration of the difficulty in tracking a problem. Even with five to ten thousand sick and about one hundred dead, the epidemic was almost missed. The reason it was discovered was that the disease was unique, acute, and came on quickly, and it still required some lucky coincidences.

Carman asks, "What would happen if a link were found between a GM food and human ill-health?" She points out that "experience with the tobacco industry indicates that affected industries tend to argue and lobby against evidence for lucrative plant products. This would be compounded by the political considerations and lobbying of many thousands of disaffected farmers whose livelihoods depended on growing the crops. . . . So, even if a GM food is found to cause harm, it may take many years of effort to remove it from the food supply."

"In short, with the level of current safety testing, if GM foods do cause human health problems, it will be very difficult to determine this, even though there may be many cases, and finding the cause and doing something about it may take decades."

Indeed, the European Commission acknowledged, "in the absence of exposure data in respect of chronic conditions that are common, such as allergy and cancer, there simply is no way of ascertaining whether the introduction of GM products has had any other effect on human health. . . . On the basis of existing research . . . it is impossible to know whether the introduction of GM food has had any human health effects other than acute toxic reactions."

4

Genetically Modified Food Is an Ethical Answer to World Hunger

Peter H. Raven

Peter H. Raven is the Director of the Missouri Botanical Garden and a member of the Pontifical Academy of Sciences, a group of scientists and mathematicians appointed by the Pope to give him counsel and advice.

Because the human population of the world is growing rapidly, and because traditional agricultural practices cannot supply enough food to support the population, it is ethically imperative that new technologies be accessed to feed the poor of the world. Humans have been modifying crops for the past 10,500 years and current gene modification techniques are no more or less safe than traditional methods of breeding crops. Studies show that the food produced is safe. In addition, genetically modified crops are less harmful to the environment than traditional agriculture. Most important, it is morally unacceptable to deny starving people safe food produced through genetic modification.

The explosive growth of the human population from 2.5 billion people in 1950 to 6.3 billion today, coupled with the desire by people around the world to achieve higher standards of living (more consumption) and the use of often unsuitable technologies has resulted in the loss of 20% of the arable land that was available in 1950. and nearly 20% of the topsoil.

Peter H. Raven, "GMOs and Science: What Have We Learned?" *AgBioWorld*, September 2004. www.agbioworld.org. Reproduced by permission.

People Are Starving

Some 700 million people, about equal to the combined populations of Europe, the United States, and Japan, are literally starving, receiving less than 80% of the UN-recommended minimum caloric intake, and therefore unable to experience proper brain development as infants or maintain their body mass as adults. As many as half of the total population of the world is malnourished with respect to one or more essential nutrients.

Half of the global population consists of people who are living on less than $2 per day. Thus there is an urgent need to achieve higher levels of productivity in agriculture everywhere to help alleviate these problems.

Any effort to deny access to technologies that are demonstrably helpful in feeding the people of the world must for this reason be judged from a moral and ethical point of view in relation to its real, not imagined, effects on human welfare. . . .

There is simply no justification for regarding imprecise traditional methods of transferring genetic traits as safe, but modern precise ones as unsafe.

Those who sidetrack new and helpful technologies on the basis of fanciful and sometimes self-serving arguments must therefore be judged in the light of the effects of their arguments on people everywhere, and not simply on the rich societies where most of those who protest the use of modern technologies enjoy lives of abundance. Colorful and threatening terms such as "contamination," "release," and "spillage" have been applied to the cultivation and dissemination of such crops, not to mention even less reasonable ones, such as "Frankenfoods" and "Terminator Genes," but these terms, which reflect a lack of logic and careful consideration, have no place in rational discourse. In the following remarks, I shall concentrate on scientific questions but also address some related considerations briefly. . . .

Genetically Modified Organisms Are Safe

First, I would like to mention that questions concerning the acceptance of genetically modified organisms (GMOs) and the problems that they might pose have been taken seriously ever since the development of recombinant DNA technologies 31 years ago (1973). Following conferences and consultations by the leading molecular biologists, careful containment of the first organisms produced by the transfer of genes from one unrelated kind of organism to another, and detailed examination of the results in hundreds of laboratories throughout the world, it has become clear that there is nothing intrinsic to the process of genetic modification by the production of transgenic organisms that makes them unsafe in any respect.

Like the many other methods that have been used to modify crops since the dawn of agriculture some 10,500 years ago, transgenic methods must be judged on the basis of their products, and not the methods by which they were produced. Idiosyncratic arguments are sometimes presented by those arguing against the adoption of GMOs, presumably for social or other reasons, but the facts reviewed by thousands of independent scientists throughout the world for three decades make this point as certain as any scientific conclusion can be. We should not therefore conduct our discussions of this matter in an atmosphere of murky, imagined threats, but rather in the light of world scientific consensus as to the safety of the methods involved. There is simply no justification for regarding imprecise traditional methods of transferring genetic traits as safe, but modern precise ones as unsafe, and we must move forward from that point as rapidly as possible.

Secondly, concerning the use of GMOs to produce food, there is no theory or set of theories that contradicts the generally accepted conclusion that those currently in use are safe as food for human beings and domestic animals, and no single case of illness resulting from consuming foods produced by GMOs, even though billions of people throughout the world use them regularly. Most beer and cheese consumed worldwide is made with the aid of GMOs, as are hundreds of different medicines.

As in the first point, arguments about the lack of safety of these foods are apparently ideologically driven, lacking a factual basis. Obviously it would be possible to produce a poisonous food with the help of gene-splicing techniques, but who would do this or put it on the market? No foods consumed by human beings are tested as extensively as those produced by GMOs, and there is no evidence of any lack of safety in such foods. To discuss these questions on the basis of an imaginary threat to human health is misleading and ought not to be acceptable to the members of a rational society.

I ... find it most distressing that the very techniques that could ... feed hungry people are so often being retarded for illogical and selfish reasons.

The Ecological Effects of Genetically Modified Organisms

Third, the ecological effects of GMOs differ according to the properties of the individual transgenic organism. Gene flow between species is a regular feature of most groups of plants, and, depending on the pollination systems of the groups involved, may extend over long distances. Studies recently reported by the U.S. Environmental Protection Agency have demonstrated the Roundup Ready genes [genes resistant to the commonly used herbicide Roundup] in bentgrass can be disseminated more than 20 km to natural populations. When wild or weedy relatives of GM crops grow near them, it can be assumed and has been widely demonstrated, that gene flow is likely to occur. . . .

There is no ecological theory that supports the idea of wild plants acquiring a transgene and then wrecking havoc in a natural community, but plenty of examples of introduced, invasive plants that have not been genetically modified playing such a role. While common sense must be a guiding principle, it is not logical to imagine consequences that have never been observed at the cost of denying people access to food or adequate economic return for their efforts. Simply to repeat the claim that widespread problems are likely to occur, or that the operation of nature is so mysterious that we can never know what will happen denies logic and flies in the face of the available facts at the cost of hungry people who deserve better treatment from those of us who are so much more fortunate than them.

I have spent my life in fostering efforts to understand biodiversity and to conserve it, and in helping to build capacity for sustainability in developing countries around the world. I therefore find it most distressing that the very techniques that could spare biodiversity and feed hungry people are so often being retarded for illogical and selfish reasons. It is unquestionably true that the development of crop agriculture, along with the domestication of animals, which began about 10,500 years ago in the eastern Mediterranean region, has been and remains extremely negative for the survival of biodiversity. The areas devoted to agriculture and grazing have grown as the human population exploded to its present 6.3 billion. Some 11% of our planet's surface is devoted to the production of crops, and an additional 20% is grazed, usually unsustainably. The "cleaner" the agriculture, the worse for biodiversity.

Agriculture Must Become More Productive

None of this in itself has anything to do with the particular genetic methods used to produce the crops, although the less land that can be cultivated for an equivalent amount of production, the better for the survival of biodiversity in adjacent areas. Nothing is more destructive to biodiversity than widespread, low-yield, traditional methods of agriculture, and it is highly misleading to romanticize them, as if all were in harmony before there were so many of us that agriculture was intensified. The extinction by Polynesians of about 1,000 species of birds (about a tenth of the world's total bird species) on the Pacific islands, along with an unknown number of other kinds of organisms, during a period about 1,200 years, offers one kind of solid evidence to the fact that all agriculture (combined in this case with hunting) is highly destructive to biodiversity. If the world's population is to be fed well, and starvation is be alleviated for the hundreds of millions of people who are suffering now, agriculture must become more productive. The development of GM crops, with precisely determined characteristics that make them survive well in the extremely diverse places that they are grown, promises major increases in productivity and a greatly enhanced ability to preserve biodiversity.

As to the reduction of diversity in the crops themselves, that is a long-term process that has little to do with the application of current methods. It is often argued that GM methods are suitable only for large-scale agriculture and that their introduction has led to the [reduced] variety in the crops, but that is simply not the case. Certainly large farms tend to have less genetic diversity in their crops than an equal area occupied by small ones, but there is no logical connection between that observation and the use of transgenic methods to produce the crops. For example, more than 500 strains of soybeans in the United States, each adapted to a particular agricultural situation have been genetically engineered, and the whole array of strains that was present initially, with all of its genetic diversity, is still being used commercially.

There is no reason in principle why minor crops grown by small-scale farmers cannot be genetically modified to make them more nutritious, better able to grow in dry or saline habitats, or whatever else is desired, thus actually helping to maintain crop genetic diversity. If smaller amounts of pesticides are applied, the case with many GM crops, the survival of biodiversity will be enhanced: for example, an estimated 70 million birds are killed by pesticide applications on croplands annually in the United States alone! Lessening the use of pesticides will also help to alleviate the estimated 500,000 cases of sickness and 5,000 deaths around the world that occur annually now as a result of the indiscriminate use of pesticides.

Despite heavy applications of pesticides, especially in Europe, there is an estimated global loss of $244 billion in crops per year, and the applications of these chemicals have serious negative consequences for the environment. In this connection, it has been estimated that if half the maize, oilseed rape, sugar beet, and cotton grown in Europe were genetically modified to resist their pests, there would be a reduction of about 14.5 million kilograms of formulated pesticide product applied, a saving of approximately 20.5 million liters of diesel, and the prevention of the emission of 73,000 tonnes of carbon dioxide into the atmosphere.

Clearly, we must develop new productive, low-input systems of agriculture, a strategy that would involve the modification of many current practices. These efforts will be aided substantially by modern genetic methods Cotton is already a global success story, and those who cultivated GM cotton are clearly better off than ever before.

In view of these considerations, it is remarkable that the major negative finding of the British study of GM crops reported in 2003 was that biodiversity was lower in the fields where GM crops were grown—because weed control was more effective there! No college of agriculture in the world teaches that it is better for productive agriculture to include more weeds, and very few places—certainly none where hungry and needy people live in the developing world—have the luxury of managing their primary fields in such a way as to encourage anything but productivity. If all of the agriculture in the world were run in such a way as to encourage weeds, there would be many more starving people, a situation that we should very much wish to avoid. Concentrating agriculture as much as possible in highly productive lands and encouraging biodiversity in uncultivated lands managed in other suitable ways is the path that we logically should follow.

As Per Pinstrup-Anderson, a leader in efforts to feed the hungry and poor people of the world, has put it, it seems natural to people in Europe and other more developed regions to use medicines produced through genetic modification but to a mother in a famine-struck region of Africa, the disease she and her children suffer from is hunger and the cure is food, The efforts of organizations such as Greenpeace to block efforts to feed people adequately throughout the world by battling biotechnology resolutely are doubtless helpful to the finances of that organization, which does not spend a cent of its money . . . to alleviate starvation or to help people, but [such efforts] are outrageous, scientifically unfounded, and should be rejected out of hand by any moral person.

It Is Morally Imperative to Feed the Needy

In our reports, we of the Pontifical Academy of Sciences stressed that it is a moral imperative for the fruits of all new technologies to be made available to all of the world's people, and more especially to those who are truly needy. Neither corporations nor wealthy nations have the right to block access to such technologies, and there is in fact a general willingness to encourage full access to them. The distribution is limited in part by the relatively small numbers of scientists in most developing countries, not much more than 10% of the world's total in the less developed countries, which include 82% of the world's people. This factor makes it difficult for many countries to evaluate on their own terms the fruits of scientific and technological advance in the rest of the world. . . .

The drive to feed hungry people and to redress the morally unacceptable imbalances . . . should take precedence over other considerations.

World trade, which is one important element that will affect the way that the growing 6.3 billion of us learn to live together, can be an instrument for good or ill depending on how it is organized. World standards are required, as are mechanisms for reaching agreements that benefit people everywhere. GMOs are one very small part of such trade, but one that has proven controversial and has been used in various ways to limit commerce. We must move to a period of reconciliation, one in which our common needs are taken into account, and not only on the basis of what is considered good in one region or another, but what the scientific and social facts may be. Doing so would allow the greater number of people to lead healthy lives that are worthy of we who live in rich countries.

The drive to feed hungry people and to redress the morally unacceptable imbalances that exist around the world should take precedence over other considerations; in this case there are no valid scientific objections to utilizing these technologies with due consideration to the implications of each new proposed transgenic crop for the environment.

The Ban on GM Foods Is Political

In conclusion, one might well ask why a general ban on GM foods and the cultivation of GM crops exists in Europe. In view of the lack of scientific evidence that such cultivation would be harmful, one can only conclude that the reasons for the ban are emotional, personal, and political. The major drop in genetic research in Europe over the past five years or so clearly has to do with this ban. Extended, it will continue to limit greatly the potentially important fruits of European research in this area and indeed to threaten the continent's economic development. Where does the gain for anyone lie in the perpetuation of this situation?

Whatever policy might be adopted for Europe persuading governments responsible for the lives of hundreds of thousands of starving people in Africa to forego food aid on the basis of politically or economically motivated disinformation seems to me to constitute a serious crime against humanity. I maintain that those responsible for this disinformation bear a responsibility for the lives of the people who are dying, and urge them to begin to deal rationally with the situation by allowing the fruits of human ingenuity to be applied to the solution of the extremely serious problem of hunger.

Loving people throughout the world in a truly Christian way demands much more of us in return for the privileges that we enjoy.

Fortunately, India and China, as well as many of the countries in Latin America, have decided to utilize GM crops to improve their economies and the nutrition of their people, which leaves Africa and some countries of South East Asia, notably Thailand, left to be pushed hard by the European Community on the issue. It is important to keep in mind that all of this controversy is taking place without a single case of human or animal sickness or environmental problem anywhere in the world reliably attributed to GM crops!

If allegations that the European Union or individual nations are funding pressure groups such as Greenpeace or "The Catholic Institute for International Relations" (not affiliated with the Vatican, and perhaps not officially with the Roman Catholic Church) are true, they clearly indicate a misuse of taxpayer funds to support ideological causes that are unsupported and harmful to the development of Europe and its individual countries.

It is exceedingly difficult to understand why public spokespeople such as former U.K. Minister Michael Meacher persist in making idiosyncratic and scientifically unfounded comments about this area. Such statements have affected a majority of European consumers and sadly led them to believe that great dangers are lurking somewhere in the practice of this particular kind of genetics. Their beliefs are doubtless sincere, but unfortunate for the future of European science and for the hungry people of the world. At any rate, for them to welcome the use of transgenic technology for beer, cheese, and drugs, while denying it to those in need of food, seems to me to be truly obscene.

Loving people throughout the world in a truly Christian way demands much more of us in return for the privileges that we enjoy.

5

Genetically Modified Food Is Not an Ethical Answer to World Hunger

Working Group on Genetic Engineering of the Justice, Peace and Creation Team

The Working Group on Genetic Engineering of the Justice, Peace and Creation Team is an advisory group to the World Council of Churches (WCC). The WCC is an organization of nearly 350 churches and denominations in 110 countries whose purpose is ecumenical Christian unity.

The use of genetically modified (GM) food seems to be a solution for the problem of world hunger. However, it is based on the assumption that industrialized agriculture is good for everyone. In reality, GM-based agriculture is good for large transnational corporations and industrialized countries, and bad for indigenous people, peasants, and small farmers. Many indigenous people view genetic engineering as abhorrent. In addition, industrial agriculture and so-called humanitarian aid that includes GM grains threaten the way of life of small farmers and the biodiversity of the planet. GM-based agriculture is not an ethical way to address hunger because it works against the values and livelihoods of people most affected.

There are currently six potential applications of genetic engineering to agriculture and food production. These are:

Working Group on Genetic Engineering of the Justice, Peace and Creation Team, "Biotechnology and Agriculture," *Genetics, Agriculture and Human Life*, Geneva, Switzerland: World Council of Churches, 2005. Reproduced by permission.

1. To increase the yields of crops—which has had little success thus far;

2. To produce crops that can withstand environmental pressures such as drought, salinity or frost—this has had little success;

3. To increase the nutritional value of the plant, so that staple legumes and cereals would carry vital amino acids, which they currently lack, thus reducing the required quantity of food intake—this process is still in its infancy;

4. To enhance resistance to disease, weeds and pests, or (as in most cases) to enhance tolerance to designer herbicides, which kill off the disease, weeds or pests but leave the plant healthy—this is the most well developed aspect of GMOs [genetically modified organisms] thus far;

5. To minimize the need for fertilizers and agrochemicals, although this seems rather unlikely as the companies which produce the GMOs also produce the fertilizers and the chemicals; and

6. To enhance the texture, flavour or shelf-life of the plant—because this could aid global trade. Quite a bit of work has been done in this area.

An Untrue Assumption

With these applications, GMOs are presented as a wonderful solution to world concerns about food security, suggesting that, with the correct application of certain techniques, hunger could be a thing of the past. Given that 15 million children below five years die each year from hunger-related causes and another 840 million people experience food shortages, the sponsors of GMOs and biotechnology naturally promote themselves as a group which cares for life and for people's livelihoods. Witness this statement which Monsanto, the giant chemical company turned life-sciences corporation, attempted to have endorsed by African leaders in 1998:

As we stand on the edge of a new millennium, we dream of a tomorrow without hunger. To achieve that dream, we must welcome the science that promises hope. We know advances in biotechnology must be tested and safe, but they should not be unduly delayed—Biotechnology is one of tomorrow's tools in our hands today. Slowing its acceptance is a luxury our hungry world cannot afford.

We are justified in asking if this is . . . just a scientific adventure which could lead us into more problems we have not even begun to anticipate.

This is a significant claim, and one that deserves the close attention of the ecumenical church which is committed to 'caring for life'. It is a claim that is made on the assumption that industrial agriculture is necessary and good. By the term 'industrial agriculture' we mean turning farms into factories through the extensive use of fossil fuels, chemicals, synthetic fertilizer, and extreme mechanization. It is sometimes referred to as 'production agriculture' in which the sole aim is the mass production of commodities. As we shall see, however, from a Christian perspective, this assumption is not true. Therefore the burden of proof as to why we should move to genetic engineering in agriculture more properly lies with its proponents than with its critics. We need now to locate GE [genetic engineering] within the wider context of the provision of food in the global context.

Genetic Engineering in Context

At the heart of the claim of the proponents of GE is the creative potential of science and technology in the service of human need, a claim that is foundational to the growth of 'western', industrialized or 'modern' society. The attempt by well-meaning or religious people to raise ethical questions about this is seen as 'superstition standing in the way of progress. Because of this, western societies hold tenaciously to the idea that technology is neutral and therefore not subject to ethical debate. However we are justified in asking if this is really about the progress of human life and community, or is just a scientific adventure which could lead us into more problems we have not even begun to anticipate.

We should remember that in its infancy western science was indeed a clear protest against power and on the cutting edge of human freedom. Science became a powerful vehicle for those who sought 'truth' over and against the established institutions of the day, among them the churches. There are many ways in which science continues to function in this way. However, it is crucial to recognise that in the context of the modern neo-liberal economic paradigm the relationship between science and power has changed significantly, so that technology is not a neutral tool, but reflects power distribution in this world and the choices made in the past by different cultures, communities and societies. . . .

The Major Actors in Genetically Modified Food

Scientists: In the past decade science, especially molecular biology and biochemistry, had to adapt to major structural changes. From publicly funded, basic science with its own ethos of intellectual honesty and transparency, it went to industry funded, narrowly specialised, so called pre-competitive research oriented towards the fast development of marketable products. Independent expertise and expertise with an appropriate level of discourse between the relevant variables, factors and fields of biological and other knowledge is not easily available in the scientific world. Some essential fields like soil ecology and structure are lagging behind. In this context, courageous, largely unprotected whistle-blowers who are willing to risk their scientific careers are the ones who lift the curtain, providing the public with essential data.

Transnational corporations and financial markets: Not only new biochemical methods of analysing anti manipulating DNA, i.e. the basis of the genetic code, but also new structures of research, development, financing and promotion are dominated by transnational corporations and financial markets. Genetic engineering technology is very expensive and consequently strives to translate general insights about the biochemical nature of heredity into speedy general application in the globalised market. It has become the driving force for the agricultural market for commodities and cash crops for export to the affluent world. This process, which undermines local farming communities and markets, has been supported by World Bank policies, and the biotech and chemical company Monsanto has become the archetype for this. Transnational corporations have the financial and political clout to use the WTO [World Trade Organization] and to persuade countries to have industry-friendly regulation, and to introduce new laws protecting the investments, property and profits of corporations, especially through patenting laws. Many faith communities and churches have naturally protested against the patenting of life forms.

Traditional and organic farmers see their way of running their farms in a holistic, low-input manner threatened.

Governments and politicians: Politicians are called to control and limit the power of players in the political arena. There are, however, enough examples for the heavy influence of major corporations and investors on the governments of the USA and other industrialised countries. Dependence on the performance of economic actors is often combined with a strong belief in the neo-liberal economic doctrine and the rhetoric of liberalisation, deregulation and privatisation, which further limits the space for political interference and action. The accelerated process of economic globalisation has made this a common concern around the globe, affecting individual countries as well as the UN System and other international bodies. . . .

Consumers: Consumers are torn between consumerism or learning to be active agents for sustainable and responsible consumption patterns. Consumers in industrialised countries usually do not make appropriate use of their purchasing power. Nevertheless consumers can play a role by insisting on GMO free food, both for their own health reasons, but also for the well-being of other communities and other generations. The fight for labelling is to be understood in this context of solidarity. In order to mobilise consumer action, the public need access to information and participation and access to jurisdiction.

Farmers and social movements: Farmers grow food for us all. The return they get for their production on the world-market is minimal compared to the benefits that trade and food processing make to their shareholders. More and more farmers around the world realise that genetically engineering their grains, tubers, nuts, fruit-trees, vegetables, salads and spices will impact on their lives. Promises of benefits at the farm-level proved only to materialise in some cases, depending on climate and socio-economic conditions, for a short period of time. Family farmers in many countries had a closer look at the situation and came up with positions of severe criticism or outright resistance. Traditional and organic farmers see their way of running their farms in a holistic, low-input manner threatened. Even industrialised farmers have come to resist decisions to grant permits for new genetically modified varieties of crops, like wheat, that will make it difficult if not impossible for them to meet consumer demands for GMO-free food.

Indigenous peoples: As soon as a culture, market, financial system, agricultural and other practices become invasive and do not allow for peaceful coexistence with other cultures and their practices, Indigenous Peoples speak up and defend their sovereignty, their land and their rights. Indigenous Peoples have clearly voiced their concerns about genetic engineering and the release of its constructs into the environment. Contamination of their traditional crops and harm to the high biodiversity Indigenous People rely on and are safeguarding would cause an irretrievable loss to their cultures.

The very development of [genetic modification] is calling into question key constants of human life and civilisation over thousands of years.

Claims About Industrial Agriculture Are Myths

The consideration of these six groups and their varied and diverse responses to the use of genetic engineering in agriculture illustrates clearly how the response is rooted in different assumptions about and experiences of industrial agriculture. The dominant actors argue that industrial agriculture is the only way to solve world hunger, and that biotechnology and genetic engineering is a natural advance on the 'green revolution'. This position can be summed up in the following seven claims:

1. Industrial agriculture will feed the world.
2. Industrial food is safe, healthy and nutritious
3. Industrial food is cheap
4. Industrial agriculture is efficient
5. Industrial food offers more choices
6. Industrial agriculture benefits the environment and wildlife
7. Biotechnology will solve the problems of industrial agriculture

A great deal of research into food security and hunger, and the experience of farmers throughout the world, has shown that these claims are myths. This growing body of international opinion is a reminder that in the area of food security, science and technology are not neutral, but are in fact rooted in the power dynamics of the global neo-liberal economic paradigm.

Listening to the Poor

It is here that we are guided by the WCC's prior commitment to understand the questions of life from the perspective 'from below', from the insights of the marginalized and those who stand in continuity with those with whom Jesus spent his life. As we do this, we take seriously the stories and voices of small-scale farmers, landless peasants and of Indigenous Peoples who do not share the assumptions made by proponents of genetically modified seeds and crops.

Growing indebtedness and despair of farming communities is a common feature around the world.

From this perspective, it is clear that biotechnology—life (*bios*) treated as, and reduced to, a matter of technology—is an expression or product of a very particular culture and time. It is not a universal project, nor is it based in universally held assumptions about what it means to be alive and to die. The very development of this technology is calling into question key constants of human life and civilisation over thousands of years. Both reproduction and production are facing changes to their very essence. Human life is itself now often thought of and used as a commodity. Food sovereignty, once the very backbone of community, is now able to be removed from the community and located in the hands of technologists and large corporations.

In many cultures, particularly of Indigenous Peoples, the idea of genetic engineering is outrageous and its practice condemned as a violent attack on life, on Mother Earth, on the Great Spirit. Genetic engineering is certainly not based on respect for the miracle of life and the integrity of the organism, whether that is a microorganism, a plant, an animal, a human being or an entire bio-habitat. Critics of this technology describe it as an expression of a monoculture that assumes nature to be alien, stingy, deficient and in need of control. Nature must be forced to surrender its 'resources', which are then transformed and improved to suit human purposes—or the purposes of some humans who control the means.

Coupled with modern capitalism, which views everything as a potential commodity, this exploitative approach to life is reinforced and determines direction and priorities of scientific research. Geared towards production of marketable and profitable commodities, science is in grave danger of being reduced to a production technique, including research and development. It becomes at the same time a political tool in the hands of commercial interests. Development of genetic research is financed as long as it continues to come up with new and potentially profitable products, from seeds to drugs to genetic 'therapies' that are protected and excluded from competition by Intellectual Property Rights. Product development is removed from critical public policy discussions with the rationalisation that we cannot stand in the way of progress and the need for companies to protect their investments in research.

Small-scale farmers in many parts of the world, Indigenous Peoples and those who care for diversity in their local habitats are vitally concerned that global agribusiness supported by the Agreement of Trade Related Intellectual Property Rights of the World Trade Organisation (WTO) and related WTO rules and regulations takes over control of seeds and indeed the whole food cycle, while exploiting their traditional knowledge and the genetic information of their own bodies They would entirely depend on the money led market economy without having the purchasing power even to buy the seeds they need to continue and to survive. Growing indebtedness and despair of farming communities is a common feature around the world. . . .

Genetically Modified Food and Humanitarian Aid

Special attention needs to be given to Food Aid, and the place of genetically engineered foods being offered to regions experiencing severe food shortages. Unfortunately, food aid is not in actuality the noble expression of solidarity and compassion as it is usually presented, but is regularly used to further political and economic interests. For example, PL480 [a food aid program] in the USA was used immediately after World War Two to create markets for US agricultural commodities such as skimmed milk powder and white flour. Research has clearly shown how such food aid (regardless of whether it is genetically modified or not) impacts upon local food production and distribution in the long run, affects local diets, and often undermines local livelihoods.

At the same time, food aid has to be critically examined as an integral aspect of support for industrial agriculture and a support for the contamination of global agriculture with GMOs. For example, the US Agency for International Development (USAID) has been the principal US agency for providing economic and humanitarian assistance to developing and 'transitional' countries since 1961. US foreign assistance has always had the furthering of America's foreign policy interests, which includes supporting the US economy, US agriculture and US trade, as a key part of its remit.

The USAID website candidly states:

> The principal beneficiary of America's foreign assistance programs has always been the United States. Close to 80% of the USAID contracts and grants go directly to American

firms. Foreign assistance programs have helped create major markets for agricultural goods, created new markets for American industrial exports and meant hundreds of thousands of jobs for Americans.

In recent years this has meant the explicit support of the biotech industry by insisting on shipping genetically engineered crops as food aid, both directly and through the World Food Programme and other agencies including the churches. USAID has been a very aggressive and explicit proponent of GMOs in food aid, and the insistence upon shipping whole grains would make it seem that deliberate contamination was and is part of the programme to undermine local agriculture and the integrity of traditional seed sources. Furthermore, once the agricultural produce from a region has become genetically contaminated through such food aid, it will weaken that nation's ability and will to establish a rigorous regulatory framework that protects agriculture in terms of its organic integrity and therefore its export possibilities.

The Ecological Consequences of Genetic Engineering

A Christian response to genetic engineering cannot ignore questions of science and power, of scientific rationality versus a relational, social rationality of life; the relationship between market and power and of the freedom of the market versus the freedom of people; the recognition of diverse ways of knowing, and of poly-culture versus monoculture. It must also face the ecological implications of genetic engineering.

While biotechnology and genetic engineering are promoted as science that offers the true epistemology of biology and biochemistry, they recognise wholeness and complexity only as an agglomeration of reducible parts or components. Organisms, including humans, are not fully recognised as having any inherent integrity, nor are clans, cultures and societies.

By understanding organisms as simply compositions of identifiable and discrete components, one can then develop a technology that can 'improve' on nature, identifying the problems it wishes to address according to solution it wishes to offer. For example, human diversity that is not seen as 'normal' has to be treated as sickness and 'cured' by means of genetic manipulation. Unintentional diversity ('weeds') in a monoculture crop must be eliminated, and genetic engineering in combination with agrotoxins is promoted as the most efficient and environmentally friendly means to that end. The fact that 'weeds' are a problem because the crop is a monoculture is excluded from consideration, because the problem might then be understood as cultural rather than technological. In this way, genetic engineering becomes a threat to biodiversity.

GMOs are an ecological threat and therefore of grave concern for those who seek to care for life on God's earth.

Genetic engineering operates on the basis of manipulating DNA from living organisms and is applied to a level of functioning in nature for which our scientific understanding is still insufficient. For this reason, precaution should be the rule, particularly since the consequences of genetic engineering are irreversible once in nature. Questions regarding gene transfer and impacts on non-target species must be adequately addressed before the products of plant biotechnology are allowed to spread. This is particularly applicable in Southern countries which possess a much greater level of biodiversity than is present in the North. . . .

The extent to which monoculture and the introduction of GE seeds will foster inequality and degradation of the natural environment in any particular economy, society or region suggests that GMOs are an ecological threat and therefore of grave concern for those who seek to care for life on God's earth.

6

Genetically Modified Food Damages Trade with Other Nations

David Kupfer

David Kupfer is a freelance journalist and photographer whose work on environmental issues has appeared in the Earth Island Journal, Progressive, *and* Whole Earth Review. *He also works for the Ecological Farming Association.*

Although large agribusinesses contend that genetically modified (GM) food crops are safe and will help preserve the environment, citizens from communities across the United States are voting on ballot initiatives designed to stop the spread of GM crops. A major issue is that GM crops contaminate conventionally grown crops by breeding with these crops. Because so many countries worldwide do not want products that contain any genetically modified organisms (GMOs), U.S. farmers have lost billions of dollars. In addition, as GMO contamination of food crops spreads, the export of U.S. food and seed will be seriously damaged.

From Mendocino, California to Montpelier, Vermont, communities are passing measures to say no to the contamination of the food supply with genetically engineered (GE) seeds and crops. Resistance to the spread of GE food crops is mounting around the country as evidence rolls in about the dangers behind GE foods and the fact that American diets have already been significantly contaminated.

The biotech industry and US government maintain that genetic engineering is a benign tool that can be used to decrease the use of herbicides and pesticides, and to improve crop yields.

"Farmers in the U.S. have lost billions . . . because of contaminated food exports and an unwillingness of foreign buyers to purchase [genetically engineered] food," says [journalist] Mark Shapiro.

Skeptics say the technology is too young for anyone to be sure of its safety, so its adoption should be slowed and monitored more closely. Evidence shows that GE foods increase the likelihood that new food allergens and toxins will be introduced into our food supply. GE crops often boost pesticide use, harming beneficial insects, earthworms, and birds. Moreover, GE crops threaten both conventional and organic farmers as a result of genetic contamination.

Farmers Have Lost Billions Because of Genetically Modified Food

"Farmers in the US have lost billions in markets because of contaminated food exports and an unwillingness of foreign buyers to purchase GE food," says Mark Schapiro, award-winning reporter with the Center for Investigative Journalism. "Those billions in lost sales translate to payouts to different farmers who make up that shortfall in agricultural subsidies from the USDA. We taxpayers are in essence subsidizing the biotech industry."

The first biotech crop went to market in 1994. Today [2004], 167 million acres worldwide are planted in biotech crops, chiefly corn, cotton, soybeans, and canola engineered to produce their own insecticides or withstand treatment by herbicides. The US is the world's top biotech crop producer.

Mendocino Says No to GMOs

Signaling a turning point in the effort to halt the introduction of genetically modified organisms (GMOs) in the US, the citizens of California's Mendocino County approved a countywide measure March 2 [2004] that prohibits the "propagation, cultivation, raising and growing of genetically modified organisms." The 56.34 percent of voters in Mendocino County who voted to ban GMOs in the county have shaken the establishment far beyond their small north coast community.

CropLife America—a national lobbying group representing agribusiness giants like [chemical companies] Monsanto, DuPont, and Dow—pumped nearly $700,000 into the campaign to defeat the initiative. The proponents of Measure H spent less than $100,000, raised mostly in small local contributions.

"This victory means the people of Mendocino County saw through the bullying of multibillion dollar corporations that were trying to undermine the democratic process. These corporations underestimated our savvy citizenry," said Els Cooperrider, a retired medical scientist, the community leader who spearheaded Measure H, and co-owner of the certified all-organic Ukiah Brewery and Restaurant.

"Mendocino County is the first GMO-free county in the nation," says local vintner Katrina Frey, co-owner of Frey Winery. "I'm sure this will motivate many other counties nationwide to mount comparable efforts."

The biotech industry is expected to challenge Mendocino's ban on the grounds that it preempts federal regulations. It also may seek to override the ban through state legislation.

Measure H was a grassroots effort in a sparsely populated county that grows no GE crops. However, Mendocino County is home to a number of wineries and vineyards, including Fetzer Vineyards, the largest grower of organic grapes in the nation.

In numerous mailers and radio ads, the corporate-funded opposition argued that the measure was poorly written and would be costly for taxpayers to enforce, requiring the county agricultural commissioner to seek out and destroy genetically modified plants—a potent threat in a county whose largest cash crop is marijuana.

Anti-GMO Activism Is Growing

On the other side of the US, Vermont senators voted 28-0 to support the Farmer Protection Act (S.164), a bill to hold biotech corporations liable for unintended contamination of conventional or organic crops by GE plant materials. Seventy-nine Vermont towns have passed measures calling on law makers in Montpelier and Washington to enact a moratorium on GMOs, and 10 percent of Vermont's conventional dairy farmers have pledged not to plant the crops.

Hawai'i is home to the highest concentration of experimental plantings of [genetically engineered] crops anywhere in the world.

More than 10 states currently have proposals for legislation against GE crops. Perhaps the most important anti-biotech action is taking shape in the Dakotas, where Monsanto plans to sell wheat that withstands the company's flagship weedkiller, Roundup. A proposal to ban GE wheat was defeated in the North Dakota Senate in 2001, but residents and farm groups are pushing a new ballot initiative.

The last year has seen a surge in GE activism across the Hawai'ian Islands, with groups working on legislative initiatives, market campaigns, Right-To-Know efforts focusing on the location of field experiments, and the creation of GE-free zones. Experimental GMO testing has been going on in Hawai'i for over a decade. Hawai'i is home to the highest concentration of experimental plantings of GE crops anywhere in the world.

The biotech industry has its sights set on California, which produces over 350 crops and is currently GE-free, with the exception of cotton grown in the Central Valley. Californians for GE-Free Agriculture is a growing coalition of farm, environmental, and consumer organizations united to prevent GE agriculture in California. The coalition is helping to form groups throughout the state that will help keep California GE free and organize locally to promote a sustainable food system.

This year [2004], the main thrust of their campaign will be stopping GE rice. In September 2003, the US EPA gave regulatory approval for Bayer's Liberty Link GE rice. Liberty Link rice is engineered to be tolerant to glufosinate, a broad-spectrum herbicide similar to Monsanto's Roundup. Liberty Link rice could be planted as soon as 2005.

The US may soon find it impossible to guarantee that ... its food supply is free of gene-altered elements, a situation that could seriously disrupt the export of US [crops].

Another company, Ventria Bioscience, gained approval March 29 to grow and mill two "pharm" varieties of rice in California on a commercial scale. "Pharm" crops are plants that have been engineered to produce pharmaceutical drugs. Ventria's "pharm" rice is engineered with human genes that produce two proteins—lactoferrin and lysozyme—used to treat iron deficiency, diarrhea, and infections in humans, and for chicken farming.

Many consumers and food companies are concerned that these and other drugs may someday end up in their breakfast cereal. The California Rice Commission's decision on allowing commercial growing of "pharm" rice is expected in the next several months.

Earlier this year, The National Research Council, an arm of the National Academy of Sciences, issued a note of caution urging more attention to methods of preventing GE plants and animals from breeding with their wild relatives.

A landmark report by the Union of Concerned Scientists (UCS) released in February shows that federal regulations have failed to prevent contamination. The report documents widespread genetic contamination of corn, soy, and canola seed stock in the US. In lab reports commissioned by the UCS, over two-thirds of 36 conventional batches of the three crops were found to contain traces of DNA from GE crop varieties.

US Exports Will Be Disrupted

If federal rules and farm practices are not tightened, UCS predicts that the US may soon find it impossible to guarantee that any portion of its food supply is free of gene-altered elements, a situation that could seriously disrupt the export of US foods, seeds, and oils.

The 70-page report, "Gone to Seed," recommends that the USDA conduct a thorough assessment of the extent of genetic contamination in the US seed industry, and that reservoirs of pure seed stocks for major crops be set aside as an "insurance policy" against the possibility of GE contamination.

7

Genetically Modified Foods Help the Environment

Nina V. Fedoroff

Nina V. Fedoroff is the Evan Pugh Professor and Verne M. Willaman Chair of Life Sciences at Pennsylvania State University. Her research has pioneered the application of molecular modifications to plants.

Human survival has historically depended on the ability to grow enough food on available acreage to feed the population. From ancient times, humans have used plant mutations to breed better food crops. Contemporary gene modification techniques allow plants to be more disease resistant, leading to decreased use of herbicides and pesticides. Genetic modifications might soon lead to plants that do not need to be treated with chemical fertilizers. The growth of the world's population requires that humans grow more food, but at the same time, the destructive effects of traditional agriculture must be curbed. Genetic modification of crops promises larger, more nutritious crops that do not harm the environment.

In chapter seven of his environmental masterpiece *Walden*, Henry David Thoreau writes about his bean field: ". . . making the yellow soil express its summer thought in bean leaves and blossoms rather than in wormwood and piper and millet grass, making the earth say beans instead of grass—this was my daily work."

Nina V. Fedoroff, "Genetically Modified Foods: Making the Earth Say Beans," *Science Journal*, Spring 2007. www.science.psu.edu/journal. Reproduced by permission of Penn State University.

The Link Between Plant Breeding and Environmentalism

You may wonder why I begin . . . with a quote from Thoreau. But to me, environmentalism and plant breeding ate inextricably linked. Our civilization rests on our ability to make the earth say beans. Other creatures feed their young, but the adults of most species fend for themselves, spending much of their day doing it. By contrast, we humans have learned to farm. Over the last few centuries, advances in science have let fewer and fewer farmers feed more and more people, freeing the rest of us to make and sell each other hats and houses and computers, to be scientists and politicians, painters, teachers, doctors, spiritual leaders, and talk-show hosts. In some parts of the world, only one person in a hundred grows plants or raises animals for food. Most of us are surprisingly unaware of what it takes to create our bread and breakfast cereal, pasta and rice, those perfect fruits and vegetables, unblemished by insect bites or fungal spots. Free to live our lives with little thought for our food, we ignore the source of the gift.

Tinkering with Nature

Our civilization rests, in fact, on a history of tinkering with nature—on making the earth say beans instead of grass. Thoreau's beans were not wild. The pod of a wild bean bursts when its seed is ripe, flinging the bean far from the parent plant to find a new place to sprout. The pods of those beans we grow for food do not burst. Such beans can no longer seed themselves. Nor can the wild grasses we have changed, over the millennia, into our staple food sources: rice, wheat, and corn. To change a wild plant into a food plant requires changes in the plant's genes. To boost its yield, to make the earth say more beans, means changing the plant's genes, as well. For thousands of years, farmers have been picking and choosing plants, propagating those with the genetic changes—mutations—that made them better food plants. Our civilization is the beneficiary of this genetic tinkering.

Jumping Genes

I have been studying plant genes—and tinkering with them— since the early 1980s, when I had the good fortune to work with Nobel Laureate Barbara McClintock, whose discovery of "transposons," popularly called jumping genes, rewrote our concept of a gene. By identifying and cloning a jumping gene in 1984, I was able to identify the DNA sequences of McClintock's transposons and then to analyze and understand how they operate. Today we know that the genome is full of transposable elements and is constantly changing. Instead of being static "beads on a string," genes can move from one chromosome to another.

Corn—maize—is one of humankind's greatest feats of genetic engineering.

Although the genes themselves are conserved over long evolutionary periods, there have been, and continue to be, numerous rearrangements, transpositions, duplications, and deletions, many of which are the work of the restless transposons. McClintock and I worked on corn, and since then I and my students have used many of the techniques of genetic engineering invented in the last 20 years to uncover the secrets of how transposons and other kinds of plant genes work. I have never applied my knowledge to making a genetically modified crop, but my familiarity with both the techniques and the corn genome made me pay attention when corporations began doing so—and when the federal government began regulating the field-testing and marketing of these crops, I have given numerous public lectures on genetically modified foods and, with co-author Nancy Marie Brown, have written the book *Mendel in the Kitchen: A Scientist's View of Geneti-*

cally Modified Foods, published in 2004 by Joseph Henry Press, an imprint of the National Academies Press.

Corn Is a Feat of Genetic Engineering

For instance, when did people begin tinkering with the genes of plants? Corn—maize—is one of humankind's greatest feats of genetic engineering. It looks nothing like a wild plant. Maize has no way of dispersing its seeds, stuck tight as they are on its enormous ears, which remain firmly attached to the plant. Scientists argued about what wild plant gave rise to maize for most of the 20th century. We now know its closest relative is a grass—teosinte. Discovered in 1896, teosinte looks so little like maize that it was assigned to a different genus: Teosinte was *Euchleana mexicana*; corn is *Zea mays*. Plants that belong to two different species (not to mention two different genera) are not supposed to cross-hybridize, but maize and teosinte do. Early genetic work by George Beadle (who would share the Nobel Prize in 1958 for the "one-gene one-enzyme" hypothesis) and his mentor Rollins Emerson of Cornell University suggested that a small number of genetic changes had transformed teosinte into maize, but it wasn't until 1992 that John Doebley of the University of Wisconsin-Madison and his colleagues, using modern molecular techniques, concluded that no more than five major genetic regions—in some cases single genes—were responsible. Changes in one of the critical genes softened the hard, silica-containing surface of the seed; another created an ear-like structure with tightly adhering seeds; and yet another telescoped a side branch into the dense husk covering the contemporary corn plant's ear.

To make corn, teosinte was genetically engineered by generations of farmers in the Balsas River basin of southern Mexico between 5,000 and 13,000 years ago. When scientists accepted teosinte as corn's ancestor, late in the 20th century, they realized the two could not belong to different genera. So they renamed teosinte: It is now a subspecies, called parviglumis, of corn, *Zea mays*.

The teosinte plant, of course, had not changed at all—only our way of naming it. The classifications "genus" and "species" are not fixed and immutable. Nor does our current definition of species particularly apply to plants. Indica rice and Japonica rice, for example, are two popular types of cultivated rice, *Oryza sativa*. They are members of the same species, and it is often difficult to tell if a single grain comes from one type or the other. Yet they do not crossbreed.

Genetic Engineering in the 1950s

Scientists in the 1950s, on the other hand, made a new, fertile grain called triticale by crossbreeding rye and durum wheat, which belong to two different genera. The secret to this early genetic engineering was colchicine, a chemical isolated from the autumn crocus. Colchicine doubles a plant's chromosomes, making the normally sterile hybrid set seeds. By the mid-1980s, triticale was grown on more than two million acres worldwide; triticale flour is commonly found in health-food stores. Colchicine is also used to make fruits seedless. A favorite fruit produced this way is the seedless watermelon.

[Genetically modified wheat] can be sprayed with a herbicide and will not die, letting farmers use energy saving no-till techniques.

Making Fruit Seedless

Another way to make seedless fruits is by using radiation to cause mutations. The Rio Red, a popular red grapefruit, was created by exposing grapefruit buds to thermal neutron radiation at Brookhaven National Laboratory in 1968. Other notable successes of mutation breeding include Creso, the most popular variety of durum wheat used for making pasta in Italy; Calrose 76, a high-yielding California rice; Golden Promise barley, a fine-quality malt used in specialty beers; and some 200 varieties of bread wheat grown around the world.

Such work is still going on. In 1996, citrus breeders Mikeal L. Roose and Tim Williams of the University of California, Riverside, irradiated budwood to develop a seedless clementine called Tango. (Generally, seedless clementines are made by spraying the flowers with a chemical that mimics a growth hormone.) By 2006, nurseries had orders for millions of Tango trees, and the researchers had extended their radiation-breeding program to include 63 varieties of citrus including mandarins, oranges, tangelos, lemons, and grapefruits.

GMOs Save Energy

In 2001, researchers at the Colorado and Texas Agricultural Experiment Stations even used radiation breeding to create a hard red winter wheat, called Above, that tolerates an herbicide produced by the BASF corporation. Above wheat can be sprayed with herbicide and will not die, letting farmers use energy-saving no-till techniques. Yet, although the end result is the same as the Roundup Ready crops sold by Monsanto, Above is not considered a "genetically modified organism" or GMO.

In fact, none of the many crop varieties created over the last 50 years through chemical or radiation mutation is considered a GMO, and they are not covered by the regulations that restrict the field-testing and sale of GM foods. In fact, they are not covered by any regulations at all, although many of the public's concerns about GM crops—such as toxicity to humans or gene flow from modified crops to wild plants— apply to these crops as well.

GMO regulations only cover plant varieties created with molecular modification techniques, which plant breeders agree are more precise and controllable—and therefore safer—than the "conventional" techniques of chemical and radiation mutation.

[GMO crops] have been found to substantially decrease farmers' use of pesticides and herbicides.

The history of molecular-modification techniques begins in the late 1960s, when molecular biologists learned to isolate and study individual genes from among the tens of thousands of genes in every plant and animal. They began to decipher the information content of different organisms, from bacteria and yeast, plants and humans, discovering that genes change rather slowly. Maize plants and humans, for example, both have hemoglobin genes that code for rather similar oxygen-binding proteins, although they use them for very different purposes. Methods were developed as well to remove and replace genes and to add new ones. With a small amount of tweaking, any gene could work in almost any other organism. The functioning of genes and cells is so similar from one organism to another that if a bacterial gene is put into a plant, it will make the very same protein it did in the bacterium. Scientists also discovered that the movement of genes from one type of organism (such as a bacterium) to another (a plant) happens in nature. Building on that discovery, scientists developed ways to systematically introduce genes into plants in order to add just the right genes to help a plant withstand nature's biological and physical stresses.

Disease-Resistant Plants

One of their first successes was in making plants disease-resistant. For example, Hawaii's papaya plantations were saved from the scourge of the deadly papaya ringspot virus by expressing just a small genetic sequence of the virus in the plant. This sentinel gives the plants the ability to recognize and destroy an infecting virus before it can reproduce, much as we immunize children against the poliovirus, but by a different molecular mechanism. Other virus-resistant varieties include a plum that can withstand the plum pox virus that ravaged Pennsylvania recently, leading the state to invest $5.1 million towards its eradication. An heirloom variety of tomato, the San Marzano (said to be the inspiration for pizza), has been made resistant to the cucumber mosaic virus; by the year 2000, that virus had wiped out 90 percent of San Marzano production in its home fields near Naples, Italy. Unfortunately, neither the virus-resistant plum nor the tomato have been planted, due to anti-GMO activism. Widespread planting in Africa of a virus-resistant sweet potato, developed by Kenyan researcher Florence Wambugu through a collaboration with Monsanto, similarly has been delayed.

GMOs Require Less Use of Pesticides and Herbicides

The most widely planted genetically modified crops are the corn and soybean varieties that tolerate herbicides, along with varieties of corn and cotton that produce an insecticidal protein from the bacterium *Bacillus thuringiensis* (Bt), long used by organic farmers to control insects. These crops, developed by a number of companies including Monsanto, Syngenta, and DuPont, have been found to substantially decrease farmers' use of pesticides and herbicides. Moreover, because they protect corn plants from invasion by certain kinds of boring insects, the fungi that follow the insects do not infect the plants, substantially decreasing the contamination of the harvested corn by harmful mycotoxins.

Healthier Food

New crops under development are focusing on making foods healthier or easier to grow, especially in harsh environments. For instance, nitrogen fertilizer would no longer be necessary if corn, wheat, and rice could fix nitrogen from the air in the way that legumes, such as peas and beans, do. Nitrogen fixation is a complex symbiosis between the legume and rhizobial bacteria that live in nodules on the plant's roots. In 2001, the DNA sequence of the rhizobial bacteria that fix nitrogen in alfalfa was published; since then more than 100 scientific studies have cited this article. A breakthrough announced by British workers in 2006 was inducing formation of the nodules without the presence of the bacteria.

In March 2007, researchers from the United States and China reported on how plants respond to the depletion of calcium from the soil, one effect of acid rain. This knowledge is a first step toward developing plant varieties that need less calcium. Other researchers are trying to make crops that are salt-tolerant, drought-tolerant, heat-tolerant, and cold-tolerant. Monsanto has identified genes that enable some plants to withstand drought and has created corn and soybean lines that grow with less water. Drought-tolerant corn is now undergoing field trials.

GMO Prevents Blindness

Researchers also are working on ways to make common foods healthier. Golden Rice, a rice that contains vitamin A, was created by Swiss researchers in 1999. The trait is currently being bred into varieties of rice traditionally grown in regions where vitamin A deficiency leads to high rates of blindness in children. In 2006, researchers in Florida reported they had bred a tomato that contains 20 times the normal amount of folate. A B vitamin, folate is needed to prevent anemia in pregnant women and birth defects in their children; lack of folate also increases the risk of vascular disease and cancer. A goal for future work is to fortify staple crops such as rice, sorghum, maize, or sweet potatoes with folate. Other researchers have made a temperate plant that produces a more-saturated, tropical-like oil which has baking properties like margarine without the transfats; a rice high in cancer-fighting flavonoids; potatoes with zeaxanthin, which wards off eye disease; and soybeans and canola oil that contain heart-healthy omega-3 fatty acids.

Oddly, these innovations aren't called plant breeding, but "genetic engineering." The new crops are not simply crops—as are the ones created using chemicals and radiation to modify plant genes—but genetically modified organisms.

Unfounded Resistance to GMOs

GMOs have met with strong resistance. Before GMOs, people might have protested the use of synthetic fertilizers or pesticides in modern farming, but they were unconcerned about whatever it was that plant breeders had done to create high-yielding hybrid corn or brilliant red grapefruits or seedless watermelons. Now, however, many people seem to agree with Britain's Prince Charles when he calls the new techniques of plant breeding "dangerous" and against God's plan.

The challenge of the coming decades is to limit the destructive effects of agriculture even as we continue to coax more food from the earth.

Part of the problem is in the words themselves. Much human effort goes into changing our environment, be it the building of highways, houses, air conditioners, shopping malls, dams, or airplanes. Although individual projects might meet with resistance, no one protests this kind of engineering. Yet the notion that plants were being engineered caught people by surprise. It was rather disquieting. Plants are, after all, natural, aren't they? Might we not be messing with Mother Nature if we began to engineer plants?

Tragic Consequences

The fantastic recent growth of electronic communication has amplified the ability to spread misinformation. Numerous organizations devote themselves to the active opposition of molecular approaches to plant breeding (though none, strangely, focus on radiation mutation, for example). Unfortunately, our understanding of scientific concepts, such as what a species is or what genes do, is often a vague mixture of fact and belief, leaving us ill-prepared to separate fact from fiction. What genetic engineering actually is and how it differs from earlier techniques of plant breeding is little known outside the laboratory and breeding plot. Our lack of knowledge could have tragic consequences. By stifling the creativity of plant breeders and by banning the results of their work from the marketplace, a "no-GMO" attitude could keep hungry people from being able to grow enough food.

The Concern of the Environmentalist

Here is my concern as an environmentalist: The human population is too large, and the Earth too small, to sustain us in the ways our ancestors lived. Most of the land that is good for farming is already being farmed. Yet 80 million more humans are being added to the population each year. The challenge of the coming decades is to limit the destructive effects of agriculture even as we continue to coax more food from the earth. Simply to provide all people living today with the same amount of food available to each American, we need to increase crop yields—unless more land is to be brought into production, which means plowing up more wilderness.

We cannot turn the clock back. At the end of the Stone Age, when most people lived in small tribes hunting wild game and gathering wild plants, the world's human population was stable at 8 to 10 million. When farming took hold as a way of life, the population began to grow. By the time of Christ, it had risen to between 100 and 300 million. When Columbus landed in the New World and the spread of food plants around the globe increased, the world's population was about 450 million. In the late 1700s, when the science of chemistry entered agriculture, it had doubled to 900 million. A century later, when Gregor Mendel's experiments were rediscovered, giving rise to the science of genetics, the population of the world was over one and a half billion.

In just the last hundred years the population doubled and redoubled. The number of people on Earth reached three billion in 1950, then jumped to six billion in little more than a single human generation. Yet farmers kept pace. Two important inventions early in the 20th century supported an enormous increase in farm productivity. First was the Haber-Bosch process for converting the gaseous nitrogen in the air to a form that plants can use as nitrogen fertilizer. Second was the observation of George Harrison Shull that intercrossing inbred corn varieties produces robust and productive offspring. This is the scientific underpinning of the entire hybrid corn industry.

Beneficial impacts [of GMOs include] the reduction in pesticide and herbicide use, the control of soil erosion through no-till farming, and the reduction in mycotoxin contamination of grain.

Geneticists Averted Famines

These inventions initially benefited the developed world. By mid-century, doomsayers were predicting famines in India and China. These famines were averted by plant geneticists, who derived mutant strains of wheat, corn, and rice that were markedly more productive than indigenous strains. From the 1960s to the 1990s, the new crop varieties and expanding fertilizer use—the Green Revolution—continued to meet the world's food needs. In 1950, 1.7 billion acres of farm land produced 692 million tons of grain. In 1992, with no real change in the number of acres under cultivation, the world's farmers produced 1.9 billion tons of grain—a 170 percent increase. If India alone had rejected the high-yielding varieties of the Green Revolution, another 100 million acres of farm land—an area the size of California—would need to be plowed to produce the same amount of grain. That unfarmed land now protects the last of the tigers.

But the human population is still expanding. And there remain places in the world where malnutrition persists and hundreds of thousands of people, especially children, die for lack of food. Where will the next increments in food production come from? I believe they will come from genetic modification.

Environmental Benefits of GMOs

Today there is widespread acceptance in North and South America for the molecular modification of crop plants, and growing acceptance in China and India. In the first decade after these crops were introduced, their adoption progressed at a remarkable pace. By 2005, genetically modified crops, primarily cotton, corn and soybeans, were being grown by more than 8.5 million farmers in 21 different countries, with no substantiated reports of adverse health effects. Beneficial impacts, on the other hand, have been substantiated by peer-reviewed scientific studies, including the reduction in pesticide and herbicide use, the control of soil erosion through no-till farming, and the reduction in mycotoxin contamination of grain.

Yet the status of crops modified by molecular techniques remains contentious in both Europe and Africa. What remains to be seen is whether the wealth of the developed countries will be deployed to the benefit of the poorest countries, where people struggle to gain a foothold on the lowest rung of the economic ladder. Molecular modification of crop plants is expensive. And yet, as some of the examples I have given . . . show, such modifications hold the promise of improving crop productivity under the most adverse climatic and biological conditions.

8

Genetically Modified Food Could Harm the Environment

Union of Concerned Scientists

The Union of Concerned Scientists is a science-based non-profit organization that conducts independent scientific research and leads citizen-based activism on issues of environmental concerns.

The long-range effects of technology on the environment are not always known when a technology is introduced. Genetically modified organisms (GMOs) might pose serious harm to humans and the environment. Such adverse effects could include, increases in allergic reactions among people consuming genetically modified (GM) foods, antibiotic resistance, and environmental toxins and fungi. In addition, GM crops can become weeds that choke out other crops and become resistant to herbicides and pesticides. They can also damage local wildlife. Just as scientists did not predict in 1939 that the pesticide DDT would endanger wildlife many years later, scientist today cannot predict the long-range environmental harm of GMOs.

Many previous technologies have proved to have adverse effects unexpected by their developers. DDT [a pesticide banned in the U.S. in 1972] for example, turned out to accumulate in fish and thin the shells of fish-eating birds like eagles and ospreys. And chlorofluorocarbons turned out to float into the upper atmosphere and destroy ozone, a chemical that shields the earth from dangerous radiation. What harmful effects might turn out to be associated with the use or release of genetically engineered organisms?

Union of Concerned Scientists, "Risks of Genetic Engineering," June 6, 2007. www.ucsusa.org. Reproduced by permission.

A Difficult Question

This is not an easy question. Being able to answer it depends on understanding complex biological and ecological systems. So far, scientists know of no generic harms associated with genetically engineered organisms. For example, it is *not* true that *all* genetically engineered foods are toxic or that *all* released engineered organisms are likely to proliferate in the environment. But specific engineered organisms may be harmful by virtue of the novel gene combinations they possess. This means that the risks of genetically engineered organisms must be assessed case by case and that these risks can differ greatly from one gene-organism combination to another.

So far, scientists have identified a number of ways in which genetically engineered organisms could potentially adversely impact both human health and the environment. Once the potential harms are identified, the question becomes how likely are they to occur. The answer to this question falls into the arena of risk assessment.

In addition to posing risks of harm that we can envision and attempt to assess, genetic engineering may also pose risks that we simply do not know enough to identify. The recognition of this possibility does not by itself justify stopping the technology, but does put a substantial burden on those who wish to go forward to demonstrate benefits. . . .

Potential Problems with Genetically Modified Crops

Transgenic crops could bring new allergens into foods that sensitive individuals would not know to avoid. An example is transferring the gene for one of the many allergenic proteins found in milk into vegetables like carrots. Mothers who know to avoid giving their sensitive children milk would not know to avoid giving them transgenic carrots containing milk proteins. The problem is unique to genetic engineering because it alone can transfer proteins across species boundaries into completely unrelated organisms.

Genetic engineering routinely moves proteins into the food supply from organisms that have never been consumed as foods. Some of those proteins could be food allergens, since virtually all known food allergens are proteins. Recent research substantiates concerns about genetic engineering rendering previously safe foods allergenic. A study by scientists at the University of Nebraska shows that soybeans genetically engineered to contain Brazil-nut proteins cause reactions in individuals allergic to Brazil nuts.

Most genetically engineered plant foods carry fully functioning antibiotic-resistance genes.

Scientists have limited ability to predict whether a particular protein will be a food allergen, if consumed by humans. The only sure way to determine whether protein will be an allergen is through experience. Thus importing proteins, particularly from nonfood sources, is a gamble with respect to their allergenicity.

The Danger of Antibiotic Resistance

Genetic engineering often uses genes for antibiotic resistance as "selectable markers." Early in the engineering process, these markers help select cells that have taken up foreign genes. Although they have no further use, the genes continue to be expressed in plant tissues. Most genetically engineered plant foods carry fully functioning antibiotic-resistance genes.

The presence of antibiotic-resistance genes in foods could have two harmful effects. First, eating these foods could reduce the effectiveness of antibiotics to fight disease when these antibiotics are taken with meals. Antibiotic-resistance genes produce enzymes that can degrade antibiotics. If a tomato with an antibiotic-resistance gene is eaten at the same time as an antibiotic, it could destroy the antibiotic in the stomach.

Second, the resistance genes could be transferred to human or animal pathogens, making them impervious to antibiotics. If transfer were to occur, it could aggravate the already serious health problem of antibiotic-resistant disease organisms. Although unmediated transfers of genetic material from plants to bacteria are highly unlikely, any possibility that they may occur requires careful scrutiny in light of the seriousness of antibiotic resistance.

In addition, the widespread presence of antibiotic-resistance genes in engineered food suggests that as the number of genetically engineered products grows, the effects of antibiotic resistance should be analyzed cumulatively across the food supply.

Toxins Pose Risks to Health and the Environment

Many organisms have the ability to produce toxic substances. For plants, such substances help to defend stationary organisms from the many predators in their environment. In some cases, plants contain inactive pathways leading to toxic substances. Addition of new genetic material through genetic engineering could reactivate these inactive pathways or otherwise increase the levels of toxic substances within the plants. This could happen, for example, if the on/off signals associated with the introduced gene were located on the genome in places where they could turn on the previously inactive genes.

There are ... environmental risks associated with the handling and disposal of the metal-contaminated parts of [genetically engineered] plants after harvesting.

Some of the new genes being added to crops can remove heavy metals like mercury from the soil and concentrate them in the plant tissue. The purpose of creating such crops is to make possible the use of municipal sludge as fertilizer. Sludge contains useful plant nutrients, but often cannot be used as fertilizer because it is contaminated with toxic heavy metals. The idea is to engineer plants to remove and sequester those metals in inedible parts of plants. In a tomato, for example, the metals would be sequestered in the roots; in potatoes in the leaves. Turning on the genes in only some parts of the plants requires the use of genetic on/off switches that turn on only in specific tissues, like leaves.

Such products pose risks of contaminating foods with high levels of toxic metals if the on/off switches are not completely turned off in edible tissues. There are also environmental risks associated with the handling and disposal of the metal-contaminated parts of plants after harvesting.

Although for the most part health risks are the result of the genetic material newly added to organisms, it is also possible for the removal of genes and gene products to cause problems. For example, genetic engineering might be used to produce decaffeinated coffee beans by deleting or turning off genes associated with caffeine production. But caffeine helps protect coffee beans against fungi. Beans that are unable to produce caffeine might be coated wtih fungi, which can produce toxins. Fungal toxins, such as aflatoxin, are potent human toxins that can remain active through processes of food preparation. . . .

Potential Environmental Harm

One way of thinking generally about the environmental harm that genetically engineered plants might do is to consider that they might become weeds. Here, weeds means all plants in places where humans do not want them. The term covers everything from Johnson grass choking crops in fields to kudzu blanketing trees to melaleuca trees invading the Everglades. In each case, the plants are growing unaided by humans in places where they are having unwanted effects. In agriculture, weeds can severely inhibit crop yield. In unmanaged environments, like the Everglades, invading trees can displace natural flora and upset whole ecosystems.

Novel genes placed in crops will not necessarily stay in agricultural fields.

Some weeds result from the accidental introduction of alien plants, but many were the result of purposeful introductions for agricultural and horticultural purposes. Some of the plants intentionally introduced into the United States that have become serious weeds are Johnson grass, multiflora rose, and kudzu. A new combination of traits produced as a result of genetic engineering might enable crops to thrive unaided in the environment in circumstances where they would then be considered new or worse weeds. One example would be a rice plant engineered to be salt-tolerant that escaped cultivation and invaded nearby marine estuaries.

Wandering Crops

Novel genes placed in crops will not necessarily stay in agricultural fields. If relatives of the altered crops are growing near the field, the new gene can easily move via pollen into those plants. The new traits might confer on wild or weedy relatives of crop plants the ability to thrive in unwanted places, making them weeds as defined above. For example, a gene changing the oil composition of a crop might move into nearby weedy relatives in which the new oil composition would enable the seeds to survive the winter. Overwintering might allow the plant to become a weed or might intensify weedy properties it already possesses.

The Harmful Resistance to Herbicides and Pesticides

Crops genetically engineered to be resistant to chemical herbicides are tightly linked to the use of particular chemical pesticides. Adoption of these crops could therefore lead to changes in the mix of chemical herbicides used across the country. To the extent that chemical herbicides differ in their environmental toxicity, these changing patterns could result in greater levels of environmental harm overall. In addition, widespread use of herbicide-tolerant crops could lead to the rapid evolution of resistance to herbicides in weeds, either as a result of increased exposure to the herbicide or as a result of the transfer of the herbicide trait to weedy relatives of crops. Again, since herbicides differ in their environmental harm, loss of some herbicides may be detrimental to the environment overall.

Squandering of Valuable Pest Susceptibility Genes

Many insects contain genes that render them susceptible to pesticides. Often these susceptibility genes predominate in natural populations of insects. These genes are a valuable natural resource because they allow pesticides to remain as effective pest-control tools. The more benign the pesticide, the more valuable the genes that make pests susceptible to it.

Engineering crop plants ... to produce plastics or pharmaceuticals could endanger mice or deer who consume crop debris ... after harvesting.

Certain genetically engineered crops threaten the continued susceptibility of pests to one of nature's most valuable pesticides: the *Bacillus thuringiensis* or Bt toxin. These "Bt crops" are genetically engineered to contain a gene for the Bt toxin. Because the crops produce the toxin in most plant tissues throughout the life cycle of the plant, pests are constantly exposed to it. This continuous exposure selects for the rare resistance genes in the pest population and in time will render the Bt pesticide useless, unless specific measures are instituted to avoid the development of such resistance.

Damage to Wildlife

Addition of foreign genes to plants could also have serious consequences for wildlife in a number of circumstances. For example, engineering crop plants, such as tobacco or rice, to produce plastics or pharmaceuticals could endanger mice or deer who consume crop debris left in the fields after harvesting. Fish that have been engineered to contain metal-sequestering proteins (such fish have been suggested as living pollution clean-up devices) could be harmful if consumed by other fish or raccoons.

The Danger of New Viruses

One of the most common applications of genetic engineering is the production of virus-tolerant crops. Such crops are produced by engineering components of viruses into the plant genomes. For reasons not well understood, plants producing viral components on their own are resistant to subsequent infection by those viruses. Such plants, however, pose other risks of creating new or worse viruses through two mechanisms: recombination and transcapsidation.

Recombination can occur between the plant-produced viral genes and closely related genes of incoming viruses. Such recombination may produce viruses that can infect a wider range of hosts or that may be more virulent than the parent viruses.

It is unlikely that all potential harms to the environment have been identified.

Transcapsidation involves the encapsulation of the genetic material of one virus by the plant-produced viral proteins. Such hybrid viruses could transfer viral genetic material to a new host plant that it could not otherwise infect. Except in rare circumstances, this would be a one-time-only effect, because the viral genetic material carries no genes for the foreign proteins within which it was encapsulated and would not be able to produce a second generation of hybrid viruses.

Additional Environmental Harm

As with human health risks, it is unlikely that all potential harms to the environment have been identified. Each of the potential harms above is an answer to the question, "Well, what might go wrong?" The answer to that question depends on how well scientists understand the organism and the environment into which it is released. At this point, biology and ecology are too poorly understood to be certain that question has been answered comprehensively.

9

Genetically Modified Food Should Not Be Banned, but Carefully Monitored

Conor Meade

Conor Meade lectures on ecology at the National University of Ireland, Maynooth.

Banning both the cultivation of genetically modified (GM) crops and the assessment of the ecological risk posed by GM crops is a bad idea. Although there are environmental and health concerns over GM food, no scientific evidence has yet determined that they are not safe. In addition, GM crops might be very beneficial and contribute to a sustainable future for all people. However, without careful study, proper decisions about the cultivation and use of GM crops cannot be made. Carefully monitored research on GM crops by public institutions is necessary. Without such research, a ban on GM crops is ill-considered.

As a dedicated home chef, as well as professional ecologist, I know that organic vegetables, poultry and dairy just taste better. What matters about this great food is not the label, or the perceived chic of paying more for your food, but rather the mentality of the organic farmer: using nature to get the best from nature. And it shows in the taste.

So it may come as some surprise that I differ from the Green Party [an Irish political party] particularly now that it is in government, when it comes to the issue of genetically modified (GM) crops.

Banning GM Research Is Short-Sighted

The proposed strategy of banning not only the cultivation, but also the ecological risk-assessment of GM crops in Ireland, is worrying and short-sighted. We should of course trade on Ireland's clean green image, as [Irish politician] Trevor Sargent said recently when launching his GM-free Ireland idea.

While European consumer sentiment is against the idea of GM, we are indeed wise to market our food produce as GM free, but the notion that we should also ban research on new crop technologies, as Sargent has suggested, is perhaps not so enlightened.

It is possible that GM food is not, in fact, bad for us at all.

There is, of course, some concern that GM crops might be harmful for us to eat. This is a legitimate concern, just as is the concern for the quality of any food we eat. However, from a scientific perspective, there is no reason to believe that GM crops should be any more harmful for us than conventional crops.

GM Foods May Be Better

Indeed from what we know about the genetic composition of edible plants, GM crops have much the same ingredients as the others—and testing their safety continues all the time. It can even be argued that certain GM crops that are resistant to, for example, herbicide or pests, are exposed to far less chemical contamination than most of the food we eat. So clearly it is possible that GM food is not, in fact, bad for us at all.

Another concern is the environment. GM crops may cross with wild relatives or grow outside cultivation, but recent evidence suggests that such is the ferocity of natural selection in wild habitats that only the leanest genomes, honed for survival over thousands of generations, can actually succeed and reproduce.

Pitted against these highly fit wild plants, cultivated crops that have been bred to rely on ample nutrient and water supplies are typically very weak. So for both conventional and GM crops, survival in the wild is just a bare possibility and successful reproduction even less likely.

GM Crops May Survive Climate Change

Certainly the variety of traits that can be bred into crops using GM technology introduces new environmental challenges. We know that climate change is drying the heart of Africa, changing countless lives along the way. There is much hope, therefore, that traits giving increased hardiness, drought resistance and salt tolerance may be introduced to staple crops, traits with a potentially huge benefit for subsistence arid-zone farmers throughout the developing world.

However, these are also the traits with the greatest potential for spread among related wild plants in the desert zone. Here we might face a potentially difficult choice between starvation and conservation. It does not mean, however, that we should ignore the potential breakthroughs that genetic modification may offer us.

There is a growing body of independent, publicly funded scientific research that suggests GM crops are not in themselves harmful to the environment.

On the other hand, herbicide-tolerant GM crops that are licensed for use in Europe really only pose a management problem for our farmers—these plants will only thrive in fields where a particular brand of herbicide is used. For plants growing anywhere else in woodlands, meadows, roadsides and sand dunes, such GM herbicide tolerance is a distinct disadvantage.

GM Crops Can Contribute to a Sustainable Future

Additionally, as we approach the progressive escalation in the cost of petrochemicals, crops which need less pesticides will begin to underpin the commercial viability of agriculture everywhere. Although GM crops are not the panacea for the ills of the developing world, if the technology is put in the hands of publicly funded institutions, it will contribute to building a more sustainable future.

The key to success lies in careful stewardship and this is where research has a critical role to play. There is a growing body of independent, publicly funded scientific research that suggests GM crops are not in themselves harmful to the environment. Put simply, making a new crop via GM methods rather than conventional crossing experiments does not make these GM crops more "risky".

What matters is the new trait that has been put into the crop, be it disease resistance, changed starch content or improved salt tolerance.

Probably the only way to put in place a durable strategy for stewardship of GM technology is not to turn our backs on it, but to come to grips with it.

European legislation will not allow crops that are potentially hazardous to the environment to be grown here and those that are judged to pose no potential harm must be managed very closely to avoid contamination of other crops. This management process, allowing conventional, organic and GM crops to be grown together, without cross-contamination, is known as co-existence.

We are at the point now of testing co-existence strategies to see if they can work, but the only way we can really do it properly is to do controlled assessments in the field. If we spurn the opportunity to validate in the field the claims made for GM crops, how can our Government stand up and be critical of these claims in Brussels?

Science may conclude at the end of the day that GM is a bad idea for us and for the environment. So be it. But what if science doesn't say this, what if it says GM has indeed great potential to benefit us and the environment, what then?

Coming to Grips with GM

Probably the only way to put in place a durable strategy for stewardship of GM technology is not to turn our backs on it, but to come to grips with it. Corporate ownership of seed patents is an issue that needs to be addressed, not least to put consumer confidence on a firmer footing. But the problem has only arisen because public science has lagged so far behind the private sector in following new opportunities.

Our public science infrastructure needs to take ownership of the issue, as [Professor] Liam Downey has pointed out. If we spurn the opportunity, then the GM issue will remain divisive for the foreseeable future.

10

Genetically Modified Food Should Be Banned

Andy Rees

Andy Rees is the author of the book Genetically Modified Food: A Short Guide for the Confused.

Many faulty arguments have been raised in favor of genetically modified (GM) crops. First, proponents say that GM crops will reduce pesticide and fungicide use. In reality, usage is scarcely reduced. Second, although proponents argue there will be little contamination of traditional crops, cross-pollination between GM crops and traditional crops is widespread. Next, the biotech industry has assured consumers that GM crops are safe. However, there are virtually no studies to support this claim. Finally, proponents argue that GM crops have gained public acceptance and offer choice. The reality is that GM crops wipe out organic farmers and have little support from consumers. The conclusion is that GM crops should be banned in the United Kingdom.

In August 2006, German chemicals company BASF applied to start GM [genetically modified] potato field trials in Cambridge [England] and Derbyshire [England] as early as next spring [2007]. The GM industry is making many claims about this product, but are these based on the truth?

Argument No. 1: We Need This Product

Late blight [a crop-damaging disease] costs UK [United Kingdom] farmers around £50m each year, even with regular ap-

Andy Rees, "GM Potatoes—Facts and Fictions," *The Ecologist*, vol. 36, no. 9, September 22, 2006, pp. 14–15. Copyright © 2006 MIT Press Journals. Reproduced by permission.

plication of fungicides. BASF claims that its GM potato would reduce fungicide spraying from around 15 times a year to just two.

The biotech industry has a long track record of first exaggerating a problem, then offering an unproven and oversold GM solution.

This sounds impressive, until you realise that just 1,300 of the 12,000 tonnes of agrochemicals used on UK potatoes are fugicides—meaning that, at most, pesticide usage would be reduced by only 10 per cent.

As far as actually reducing pesticide usage is concerned, Robert Vint of Genetix Food Alert observes that "such claims ... usually [soon] prove to be extreme exaggerations". The biotech industry has a long track record of first exaggerating a problem, then offering an unproven and oversold GM solution. A classic example of this was [chemical company] Monsanto's showcase project in Africa, the GM sweet potato. It was claimed that the GM potato would be virus resistant, that it would increase yields from four to 10 tonnes per hectare, and that it would lift the poor of Africa out of poverty. However, this crop not only wasn't virus-resistant, but yielded much less than its non-GM counterpart. Moreover, the virus it targeted was not a major factor affecting yield in Africa. The claims were made without any peer-reviewed data to back them up. And the assertion that yields would increase from four to 10 tonnes per hectare relied upon a lie—according to FAO [Food and Agriculture Organization] statistics, non-GM potatoes typically yield not four but 10 tonnes. Furthermore, a poorly resourced Ugandan virus-resistant sweet potato, that really was roughly doubling yields, was studiously ignored by the biotech lobby.

Also conveniently overlooked are any non-GM solutions to blight. Many conventional potato varieties are naturally blight resistant, some of which the organic sector are currently trialling. Another non-GM control, used by organic farmers against late blight in potatoes, is the use of copper sprays in low doses. This is applied to the foliage of the plant and does not contaminate the tuber.

Argument No. 2: Minimal Contamination

An article in *The Guardian*, which reads more like a BASF press release . . . , reports that "Andy Beadle, an expert in fungal resistance at BASF, said the risks of contamination from GM crops are minimal because potatoes reproduce through the production of tubers, unlike other crops such as oil seed rape [canola], which produces pollen that can be carried for miles on the wind."

Not only is this remark economical with the facts, it seems a little brazen given the biotech industry's rather prolific history on contamination issues, which has resulted in at least 105 contamination incidents (some of them major), over 10 years, and in as many as 39 countries.

Amongst many other things, Mr Beadle forgot to mention that there is less direct risk of contamination by cross-pollination, not no risk. Furthermore, cross-pollination is much higher when the GM and non-GM potato varieties are different; one study showed that, even at plot-scale, 31 per cent of plants had become hybrids as far as 1 km [kilometer] from a GM variety. Cross-pollination also increases greatly when the chief pollinator is the 'very common' pollen beetle, which travels considerably further than another potato pollinator, the bumble bee. Years later, cross pollination is still possible through potato volunteers (plants from a previous year's dropped tubers or seed); Defra [United Kingdom Department for Environment Food and Rural Affairs] itself has acknowledged this problem. And similarly, 'relic' plants can persist in fields or waste ground. What is more, blight-resistant varieties create a far greater risk of GM contamination because the flowering tops are more likely to be left on than with non-blight-resistant varieties. This is because tops are usually removed from non-blight-resistant varieties to reduce disease incidence. Also, a number of modern strains can produce considerable numbers of berries, each producing 400 seeds; these can lay dormant for seven years, before becoming mature tuber-producing plants.

In October 2000, in the US, GM StarLink corn, approved only as animal feed, ended up in taco shells and other food products.

And if all that isn't enough to suggest that 'minimal' contamination is the figment of the corporate imagination, then it is well worth checking out the March 2006 GM Contamination Register, set up by Greenpeace and GeneWatch UK. . . . This includes some of the worst contamination incidents to date, including the following three.

In October 2000, in the US, GM StarLink corn, approved only as animal feed, ended up in taco shells and other food products. It led to a massive recall of more than 300 food brands and cost Aventis [an international pharmaceutical company] an immense $1 billion to clear up. StarLink corn was just one per cent of the total crop, but it tainted 50 per cent of the harvest. In March 2005, Syngenta [an international agribusiness] admitted that it had accidentally produced and disseminated—between 2001 and 2004—'several hundred tonnes' of an unapproved corn called Bt10 and sold the seed as approved corn, Bt11. In the US, 150,000 tonnes of Bt10 were harvested and went into the food chain. And in April 2005, unauthorised GM Bt rice was discovered to have been sold and grown unlawfully for the past two years in the Chinese province of Huber. An estimated 950 to 1200 tons of the rice entered the food chain after the 2004 harvest, with the risk of up to 13,500 tons entering the food chain in 2005. The rice may also have contaminated China's rice exports. And now, in 2006, BASF's application comes amidst the latest biotech scandal, that of US rice contamination by an unauthorised, experimental GM strain, Bayer's LLRice 601.

Argument No. 3: Separation Distances

The GM lobby have proposed a buffer zone of 2-5m [meters] of fallow land around the GM potato crop, together with a 20m separation with non-GM potato crops.

The National Pollen Research Unit (NPRU), on the other hand, has recommended separation distances of 500m. Interestingly, pro-industry sources have always claimed that only very small separation distances are necessary, with buffer zones for rape set at a derisory 200m in the UK crop trials. Judith Jordan (later Rylott) of AgrEvo (now Bayer) gave evidence under oath that the chances of cross pollination beyond 50m were as likely as getting pregnant from a lavatory seat. Well, you have been warned. But oilseed rape pollen has been found to travel 26km, maize [corn] pollen 5km, and GM grass pollen 21km.

The truth is that, as far as human health goes, the biotech industry cannot know that their products are safe, because there has only been one published human health study.

Meanwhile, good ol' Defra is once again paving the way for the biotech industry, with its so called 'co-existence' paper of August 2006. This will determine the rules for commercial GM crop growing in England—yet astonishingly, it proposes no separation distances. GM contamination prevention measures will be left in the slippery hands of the GM industry in the form of a voluntary code of practice.

Argument No. 4: This Product Is Safe

The biotech industry has from the very beginning assured us that their products are entirely safe. This is because, they claim, they are so similar to conventional crops as to be 'Substantially Equivalent', a discredited concept that led to GM crop approval in the US (and thence the EU [European Union]).

The truth is that, as far as human health goes, the biotech industry cannot know that their products are safe, because there has only been one published human health study—the Newcastle Study, which was published in 2004 And although this research project was very limited in scope, studying the effects of just one GM meal taken by seven individuals, it nonetheless found GM DNA transferring to gut bacteria in the human subjects.

In Canada, . . . the organic canola industry was pretty much wiped out by GM contamination.

As for tests of the effects of GM crops on animals, there are only around 20 published studies that look at the health effects of GM food (not hundreds, as claimed by the biotech lobby), as well as some unpublished ones. The findings of many of these are quite alarming. The unpublished study on the FlavrSavr tomato [a GM tomato] fed to rats, resulted in lesions and gastritis, in these animals. Monsanto's unpublished 90-day study of rats fed MON863 maize resulted in smaller kidney sizes and a raised white blood cell count. And when it comes to GM potatoes, Dr Ewen and Dr Pusztai's 1999 10-day study on male rats fed GM potatoes, published in the highly respected medical journal *The Lancet*, showed that feeding GM potatoes to rats led to many abnormalities, including: gut lesions; damaged immune systems; less developed brains, livers, and testicles; enlarged tissues, including the pancreas and intestines; a proliferation of cells in the stomach and intestines, which may have signalled an increased potential for cancer; and the partial atrophy of the liver in some animals. And this is in an animal that is virtually indestructible.

Argument No. 5: Increasing Choice

The proposed UK trials would follow those being carried out in Germany, Sweden and the Netherlands. Barry Stickings of BASF explains: "We need to conduct these [in the UK] to see how the crop grows in different conditions. I hope that society, including the NGOs [non-governmental organizations] realise that all we are doing is increasing choice."

So, how much choice has GM crops given farmers? Well, in Canada, within a few years, the organic canola industry was pretty much wiped out by GM contamination. And in the US, a 2004 study showed that, after just eight years of commercial growing, at least 50 per cent of conventional maize and soy and 83 per cent of conventional canola were GM-contaminated—again dooming non-GM agriculture.

In the U.S., . . . GM potatoes were taken off the market . . . when McDonald's, Burger King, McCain's and Pringles all refused to use them, for fear of losing customers.

Argument No. 6: Public Opinion

Regarding BASF's application to trial GM potatoes, the *Financial Times* reported that "Barry Stickings of BASF said he did not expect too much opposition to the application". What had clearly slipped Stickings' mind was that BASF had already faced protests with this product in Sweden, where it is in its second year of production.

In Ireland, where one may have expected more enthusiasm for the project, given the history of blight during the 1840s famine, BASF was given the go ahead earlier this year for trials of its GM blight-resistant potato, only to face stiff public resistance and rigorous conditions enforced by the Irish Environmental Protection Agency. BASF later discontinued the trials.

In the UK and Europe, as Friends of the Earth points out: "Consumers . . . have made it clear that they do not want . . . GM food". In fact, the British Retail Consortium, which represents British supermarkets, has already stated that they 'won't be stocking GM potatoes for the conceivable future' because 'people remain suspicious of GM'. My forthcoming book goes into the rejection of GM crops in more depth.

And even more surprisingly, in the US, where 55 per cent of the world's GM crops are grown, GM potatoes were taken off the market back in 2000 when McDonald's, Burger King, McCain's and Pringles all refused to use them, for fear of losing customers.

Conclusion: Ban GM Crops

So, having reviewed the claims made about BASF's GM potatoes, and having found them, well, somewhat lacking, there is only one course of action open to the government, and that is, as Friends of the Earth's GM Campaigner Liz Wright recently said, to ". . . reject this application and prevent any GM crops from being grown in the UK until it can guarantee that they won't contaminate our food, farming and environment."

Organizations to Contact

The editors have compiled the following list of organizations concerned with the issues debated in this book. The descriptions are derived from materials provided by the organizations. All have publications or information available for interested readers. The list was compiled on the date of publication of the present volume; the information provided here may change. Be aware that many organizations take several weeks or longer to respond to inquiries, so allow as much time as possible.

AgBioWorld
P.O. Box 85, Tuskegee Institute, AL 36087-0085
(334) 444-7884
Web site: www.agbioworld.org

The AgBioWorld Foundation is a non-profit organization run by Professor C.S. Prakash of Tuskegee University. The Foundation's goal, according to their own literature, is to provide science-based information on agricultural biotechnology to people around the world. They publish an electronic newsletter *AgBioView* that is very useful for any student of genetically modified food. Their Web site maintains archives of the newsletter as well as additional research articles and links.

American Institute of Biological Sciences
1444 Eye St. NW, Suite 200, Washington, DC 20005
(202) 628-1500
Web site: www.aibs.org

The American Institute of Biological Sciences is a non-profit organization of scientists and researchers dedicated to advancing biological research and education for the welfare of society. They maintain the ActionBioscience.org Web site as an educational resource. The Web site provides peer reviewed articles and links on each of the following: biodiversity, the environment, genomics, biotechnology, evolution, new frontiers, and education.

The Campaign to Label Genetically Engineered Food
P.O. Box 55699, Seattle, WA   98155
(425) 771-4049
E-mail: label@thecampaign.org
Web site: www.thecampaign.org

The Campaign to Label Genetically Engineered Food is an advocacy group that lobbies Congress and the President of the United States to pass legislation that will require the labeling of genetically modified food in the United States. On its Web site, the organization offers information about pending legislation, opportunities for activism, and educational resources regarding food labeling.

Christian Ecology Link
CEL Information Officer, 3 Bond Street
Lancaster   LA1 3ER
   UK
+44 (0) 1524 36241
E-mail: info@Christian-ecology.org.uk
Web site: www.Christian-ecology.org.uk

The Christian Ecology Link organization is a non-denominational religious group that gathers and provides information on environmental concerns. They use Christian principles to formulate their arguments for or against particular issues. In addition, they provide suggestions for action. The group publishes leaflets and pamphlets in addition to maintaining a well-organized, informative Web site.

Bill & Melinda Gates Foundation
P.O. Box 23350, Seattle, WA   98102
(206) 709-3100
E-mail: info@gatesfoundation.org
Web site: www.gatesfoundation.org

The Bill & Melinda Gates Foundation is a philanthropic foundation begun by the founder of Microsoft and his wife. The Foundation supports a number of causes throughout the world, including the development of Golden Rice. The Web site has many articles and links describing the uses of genetically modified food to answer the problem of world-wide hunger.

Greenpeace

702 H Street, NW, Washington, DC   20001
(202) 462-1177
E-mail: info@wdc.greenpeace.org
Web site: www.greenpeace.org

Greenpeace is a widely known, nonprofit environmental advocacy organization. Greenpeace strongly opposes the development and dissemination of genetically modified seed and food. On their Web site, readers will find many arguments against GMOs as well as articles, news releases, and research materials.

HarvestPlus

c/o IFPRI, 2033 K Street, NW, Washington, DC   20006-1002
E-mail: B.McClafferty@CGIAR.org
Web site: www.harvestplus.org

HarvestPlus is a world-wide group of scientists and institutions whose goal is to breed new varieties of food to address the nutritional needs of all people. Their stated purpose is to increase the nutrients in food through a process called "biofortification." Their Web site has many publications, articles, links, and research reports useful for the study of genetically modified food.

IMPACT (International Marketing Program for Agricultural Commodities and Trade)

P.O. Box 646214, Pullman, WA   99154-6214
(509) 335-6653
Web site: www.impact.wsu.edu

IMPACT is a program sponsored by Washington State University whose goal, according to their Web site, "is to use advances in science to improve the competitiveness of food and agricultural systems in today's global market." The program is a source of essays, articles, and news briefs concerning genetic engineering and food.

The Institute for Agriculture and Trade Policy
2105 First Avenue South, Minneapolis, MN   55404
(612) 0870-0453 • Fax: (612) 870-4846
E-Mail: iatp@iatp.org
Web site: www.iatp.org

The Institute for Agriculture and Trade Policy is an advocacy group promoting family farms and rural communities through research, science, and education. Their primary concerns include helping family farms withstand growing globalization. In addition, they advocate for sustainable agriculture that produces safe food and maintains a healthy environment. The organization maintains a Web site that includes articles, publications, press releases, and editorials.

The Institute for Responsible Technology
P.O. Box 469, Fairfield, IA   52556
(641)209-1765
E-mail: info@ResponsibleTechnology.org
Web site: www.ResponsibleTechnology.org

The stated goal of this organization is to "end the genetic engineering of our food supply." Its founder, Jeffrey M. Smith, is a well known opponent of genetic engineering. The Institute's Web site has many articles and links to useful resources. In addition, it offers a free, monthly e-newsletter called *Spilling the Beans.*

The Institute of Science in Society
P.O. Box 51885, London   NW2 9DH
  UK
44 20 8452 2729
Web site: www.i-sis.org.uk

The Institute of Science in Society is a non-profit organization based in London that advocates ecological sustainability and social accountability. The organization opposes the use of genetically modified food, claiming that it is "inherently hazardous to health." Available on the group's Web site are many articles and publications. In addition, they offer for sale a dossier of 160 referenced articles on genetic modification.

Monsanto Company
800 N. Lindbergh Blvd., St. Louis, MO 63167
(314) 694-1000
Web site: www.monsanto.com

Monsanto is a multinational agricultural biotechnology corporation. They are one of the leading companies supporting the research and development of genetically modified food crops in order to ensure the success of farmers. Their Web site offers a wide variety of news, research articles, and other materials to help consumers and students understand the field.

The National Centre for Biotechnology Education (NCBE)
Science and Technology Centre, Earley Gate, The University
    of Reading, Whiteknights, Reading   RG6 6BZ
    The United Kingdom
+44 (0) 11 89 87 37 43 • Fax: +44 (0) 11 89 75 01 40
E-Mail: NCBE@reading.ac.uk
Web site: www.ncbe.reading.ac.uk

The NCBE has been in existence for the past twenty-five years and is a part of the University of Reading in the United Kingdom. The Centre is self-supporting through the sales of course materials and teacher training. It is not an advocacy organization and does not participate in lobbying to influence public policy, nor does the Centre take a stand on the issue of GM food. Their Web site attempts to present literature on all sides of the debate free of charge. The Centre offers a host of articles and analyses of important technological issues, including GM food.

Society, Religion, and Technology Project (SRT)
Church of Scotland, 121 George Street, Edinburgh   EH2 4YN
    Scotland

0131-240-2250 • Fax: 0131-240-2239
E-mail: srtp@srtp.org.uk
Web site: www.srtp.org.uk

The Church of Scotland's Society, Religion and Technology Project exists to provide current information on many key ethical issues so that church members can make their own decisions about their involvement in such issues. On their Web site, the SRT includes multi-disciplinary, well researched articles and materials. Their book, *Engineering Genesis*, offers a balanced view of genetic engineering. A link to the book is available on the Web site.

World Health Organization (WHO)
Avenue Appia 20, Geneva 27   CH - 1211
  Switzerland
+41 22 791-2111
Web site: www.who.int

The WHO directs and coordinates health initiatives for the United Nations system. According to the WHO Web site, the organization is responsible for "providing leadership on global health matters, shaping the health research agenda, setting norms and standards, articulating evidence-based policy options, providing technical support to countries, and monitoring and assessing health trends." On their Web site, the WHO maintains a large section of literature on the safety of GMOs.

Bibliography

Books

Dominique Brossard and James Shanahan	*The Media, the Public and Agricultural Biotechnology*, Cambridge, MA: CABI, 2007.
Guy Cook	*Genetically Modified Language*, London and New York: Routledge, 2004.
Craig Donnellan	*Genetic Modification*, Cambridge, UK: Independence, 2004.
Jon Entine	*Let Them Eat Precaution: How Politics Is Undermining the Genetic Revolution in Agriculture*, Washington, DC: AEI Press, 2006.
John Farndon	*From DNA to GM Wheat: Discovering Genetic Modification of Food*, Oxford: Heinemann Library, 2006.
Nina Federoff and Nancy Marie Brown	*Mendel in the Kitchen: A Scientist's View of Genetically Modified Foods*, Washington, DC: Joseph Henry Press, 2004.
Michael W. Fox	*Killer Foods: When Scientists Manipulate Genes, Better Is Not Aways Best*, Guildford, CT: Lyons Press, 2004.
Vicky Franchino	*Genetically Modified Food*, Ann Arbor, MI: Cherry Lake Publishing, 2006.

Jen Green	*Everything You Wanted to Know about GM Food*, London: Watts, 2004.
Moira Anne Gunn	*Welcome to BioTech Nation: My Unexpected Odyssey into the Land of Small Molecules, Lean Genes, and Big Ideas*, New York: AMACOM, 2007.
N. G. Halford	*Plant Biotechnology: Current and Future Applications of Genetically Modified Crops*, Hoboken, NJ: J. Wiley, 2006.
R.A. Hindmarsh, and Geoffrey Lawrence	*Recoding Nature: Critical Perspectives on Genetic Engineering*, Sydney, Australia: UNSW Press, 2004.
Daniel Lee Kleinman and Abby J. Kinchy	*Controversies in Science and Technology: From Maize to Menopause*, Madison, WI: University of Wisconsin Press, 2005.
Michael D. Mehta	*Biotechnology Unglued: Science, Society, and Social Cohesion*, New York: Routledge, 2004.
Marion Nestle	*Safe Food: Bacteria, Biotechnology, and Bioterrorism*, Berkeley, CA: University of California Press, 2004.
Peter Pringle	*Food, Inc.: Mendel to Monsanto—The Promises and Perils of the Biotech Harvest*, New York: Simon and Schuster, 2005.
Andy Rees	*Genetically Modified Food: A Short Guide for the Confused*, Ann Arbor, MI: Pluto Press, 2006.

Reinhard Renneberg and A.L. Demain	*Biotechnology for Beginners*, Boston, MA: Academic Press, 2008.
Pamela C. Ronald and Raoul W. Adamchak	*Tomorrow's Table: Organic Farming, Genetics, and the Future of Food*, New York: Oxford University Press, 2007
Jeffrey M. Smith	*Genetic Roulette: The Documented Health Risks of Genetically Engineered Foods*, Fairfield, IA: Yes! Books, 2007.
Claire Stanford	*World Hunger*, Bronx, NY: H.W. Wilson Company, 2007.
Dave Toke	*The Politics of GM Food*, London: Routledge, 2004.

Periodicals

Fatima Agha Al-Hayani	"Biomedical Ethics: Muslim Perspectives on Genetic Modification," *Zygon*, March 2007.
William Alexander	"It Isn't Easy Being Organic: The Herbivore's Dilemma," The *International Herald Tribune*, May 30, 2006.
Britt Bailey and Becky Tarbotten	"Turning Point for Californian's Farm Industry," *San Francisco Chronicle*, July 20, 2005.
Jerry Cayford	"Breeding Sanity into the GM Food Debate," *Isssues in Science and Technology*, Winter 2004.

Ross Clark
"What's Good for GM Is Good for the World," *The Spectator*, October 25, 2003.

Gerald D. Coleman
"Is Genetic Engineering the Answer to Hunger?" *America*, February 21, 2005.

Elena Conis
"Biotech Buffet: Folate-Rich Tomatoes, Hypoallergenic Peanuts, Heart-Healthy Soybean Oil. The Next Wave of Genetically Engineered Food Is Coming—But Will We Bite?", *Los Angeles Times*, October 22, 2007.

Elizabeth Cullen
"We Are the Guinea Pigs in GM Food Trials," *The Irish Times*, May 17, 2006.

Jenninfer Cutraro
"Consumers Value Genetically Modified Foods That Directly Benefit Them," *Purdue [University] News*, October 24, 2003.

East African
"Kenya: How New Food Crops Are Being Forced Down Our Throat," July 10, 2007.

Derek Hanekom
"Cautiously Sowing the Seeds of Change," *Business Day (South Africa)*, August 2, 2006.

John Hepburn
"Asia's Looming Biotech Food Fight," *Eastern Economic Review*, June 2005.

Julian Little and Bernard Marantelli
"GM Is Safe and That's a Fact," *Chemistry and Industry*, July 4, 2005.

Robin Maynard and Pat Thomas — "The Next Genetic Revolution?" *The Ecologist*, March 2007.

Shiri Pasternak — "Stories from Guatemala and North America: Why Indigenous Beliefs Matter in the Debate on Genetically Engineered Food," *Health Law Review*, Fall 2006.

John Pickrell — "Instant Expert: GM Organisms," *New Scientist*, September 4, 2006.

Trey Popp — "God and the New Foodstuffs," *Science and Spirit*, March 2006.

C.S. Prakash and Gregory Conko — "Technology That Will Save Billions from Starvation," *The American Enterprise*, March 1, 2004.

Arpad Pusztai — "We Can't Ignore GM Concerns," *Chemistry & Industry*, August 15, 2005.

Jeremy Rifkin — "Beyond Genetically Modified Crops," *The Washington Post*, July 4, 2006.

Charles W. Schmidt — "Genetically Modified Foods: Breeding Uncertainty," *Environmental Health Perspectives*, August 2005.

Gyorgy Scrinis — "Food Production Must Not Be Controlled by a Few Corporations," *The Age*, August 17, 2007.

Jeffrey M. Smith — "Cause for Concern," *The Ecologist*, October 2005.

Graham
Thompson
"Debate: Genetically Modified Food and the WTO Ruling," *Ethical Corporation*, April 4, 2006.

Jennifer A.
Thomson
"Use Biotechnology to Feed the Poor," *The Australian*, February 7, 2006.

Lisa Turner
"Playing with Our Food," *Better Nutrition*, April 2007.

US Newswire
"Food Supply Vulnerable to Contamination by Drugs and Plastics from Gene-Altered Crops," December 15, 2004.

Laylah Zurek
"The European Communities Biotech Dispute: How the WTO Fails to Consider Cultural Factors in the Genetically Modified Food Debate," *Texas International Law Journal*, Spring 2007.

Index